GEMS

An Introduction to Canadian Buddhism
for Young People and the Young at Heart

Kenneth K. Tanaka
with Durgesh Kasbekar and John H. Negru

Gems
An Introduction to Canadian Buddhism
for Young People and the Young at Heart
Kenneth K. Tanaka, Durgesh Kasbekar, and John H. Negru

Published by
The Sumeru Press Inc.
PO Box 75, Manotick Main Post Office,
Manotick, ON, Canada K4M 1A2

Copyright © 2022 by Kenneth K. Tanaka
Chapters 1 & 5 Copyright © 2022 by Durgesh Kasbekar
Chapter 2 Copyright © 2022 by John H. Negru
Paintings in Chapter 3 by K. Nousu. Courtesy of BDK
   (The Society for the Promotion of Buddhism)
Cartoons Copyright © 2019 by Jon J. Murakami
Images on pages 89 & 160 by Rev. Ken Sugahara, Tokyo, Japan
Cover photo courtesy of Joyce Lam

ISBN 978-1-896559-84-1

All rights reserved. No part of this book may be reproduced, stored in a retrieval system, or transcribed in any form or by any means—electronic, mechanical, photocopying, recording, or otherwise—without the prior written permission of the publisher.

LIBRARY AND ARCHIVES CANADA CATALOGUING IN PUBLICATION

Title: Gems : an introduction to Canadian Buddhism for young people and the young at heart / Kenneth K. Tanaka ; with Durgesh Kasbekar and John H. Negru.
Other titles: Introduction to Canadian Buddhism for young people and the young at heart
Names: Tanaka, Kenneth Ken'ichi, author. | Kasbekar, Durgesh, author. | Negru, John, author.
Identifiers: Canadiana 20220245517 | ISBN 9781896559841 (softcover)
Subjects: LCSH: Buddhism—Canada.
Classification: LCC BQ742 .T36 2022 | DDC 294.30971—dc23

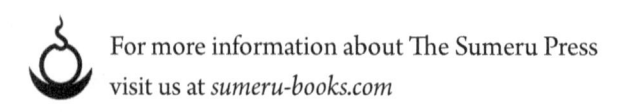

For more information about The Sumeru Press visit us at *sumeru-books.com*

*To Buddhist youth and young adults
on whose shoulders the future of
Canadian Buddhism rests*

Contents

Preface 7
Introduction 11

Part One: Here and Now
1. Buddhism in Canada 17
2. Living Buddhist Experience in Canada 29

Part Two: Legacy
3. Life of the Buddha .41
4. Brief History of Buddhism in Asia 51
5. Brief History of Buddhism in Canada 65

Part Three: Basic Teachings and Practices with Humour and Light-hearted Stories
6. Four Noble Truths 77
7. Karma and the Eightfold Noble Path 87
8. Four Marks of Life 99
9. Popular Passages, Metaphors, and Stories 107

Part Four: In Daily Life
10. Issues and Problems in Daily Life 121
11. Questions Often Asked about Buddhism 133
12. Humour as a Way to Learn and Share Buddhism 139

Epilogue 155

Appendices
I: Important Dates in Buddhism and Christianity 157
II: Buddhists in the World 158
III: Relating to Other Religions 159
IV: Buddhist Holidays 161

Photo Section 163
About the Authors 175
Index 179

Preface

The Coming of Age of Buddhism in North America

LET'S BEGIN BY SHARING a funny cartoon that I once saw in a newspaper.[1]

A Christian on a busy city sidewalk is carrying a placard that reads: "Jesus is coming!"

Behind him there is a Buddhist monk, smiling and carrying a placard of his own that reads:

"Buddha HERE NOW!"

This symbolizes, for me, the coming of age of Buddhism as a *North American* religion. This Buddhist is proudly—and even in a challenging manner—expressing Buddhist teaching on an *equal* footing with the Christian. Further, over 35 million people or one-tenth of the population in Canada and the United States are either Buddhists, Buddhist sympathizers, or have been strongly influenced by Buddhism.

Challenges of Being a Young Buddhist

However, this was not always the case. For me, growing up Buddhist in California in the early 1960s was not easy. There were very few Buddhists around, and many people looked at Buddhism as some Asian cult where followers meditated by staring at each other's belly buttons!

So, it was not easy being a young Buddhist in those days. Fortunately, things have changed enormously since then. Buddhism is today much more well known, and, as I will show in this book, it is now a "North American religion" and no longer just a religion of Asia. Further, there are now far more "famous" Buddhists, great books on Buddhism, and information available on the Internet.

---

1. *San Francisco Examiner*, in July 1987. The wording is the same, but the cartoon was newly created for this book.

A Book for Youth and Young Adults

Despite this, I feel there are very few introductory books for youths and young adults on Buddhism. That motivated me to work on an easy-to-understand introductory book for this audience. I feel I can accomplish this because of my own background of having been a Buddhist *youth*. Plus, I have raised three Buddhist young adults.

It is my strong wish to contribute to the well-being of North American youth who are Buddhists or interested in Buddhism. So, the book is not only for those whose families are Buddhist but also for those who are personally attracted to Buddhism. Despite the growth of Buddhism in this country, there are still many challenges of living in a society dominated by Christian and, to some extent, Jewish values and customs. For example, many of our politicians take oaths of office by placing their hands on the Bible and often end their speeches invoking God to protect the country.

Buddhism comes in many forms, for there are hundreds of denominations from numerous countries of Asia. What is fascinating about North American Buddhism is that Los Angeles, Vancouver, Chicago, Toronto and other metropolitan areas have more different kinds of Buddhist denominations than are found in any large city in Asia, including Bangkok, Taipei, Seoul, and Kyoto. For the first time in the 2,600 years of Buddhist history, virtually *all* the major Buddhist denominations in the world today are co-existing in many of the largest North American metropolitan areas. It's exciting to be living in such a remarkable setting and time!

In this book, I have tried to find commonality among these multiple denominations by focusing on the *early* Buddhist teachings before the formation of denominations took place. By so doing, we are able to present a set of teachings and practices that are *common* to all the traditions. This book or any one book, for that matter, cannot cover and do justice to the distinct features of the many Buddhist denominations. For that, you are asked to consult the resources provided by each of the denominations.

Acknowledgements

Being of the Baby Boomer generation, I needed the eyes of the younger generation to look through the manuscript of this book. I was, therefore, so pleased when a group of young people responded to my request by offering valuable suggestions. So my heartfelt appreciation goes to Leah Chase, Harrison Chin, Joshua McKinney, Kelli and Sarah Matsumura, Naho Umitani, and Jason Yokoyama. With such committed and knowledgeable young people, I am even more hopeful for the future of North American Buddhism.

I wish also to thank the members of the various communities that make up the kaleidoscope of North American Buddhist traditions. Allow me to make special mention of those who gave me encouragement to pursue this book project: Bishop Tatsuya Aoki, Mr. Greg Chor and Mrs. Laura Sugimoto (Jodo Shinshu Buddhist Temples of Canada); Rev. Tu Luc (Chua Pho Tu Temple – Vietnamese tradition); Rev. Bhante Seelawimala (Theravada – Sri Lankan tradition); Rev. Marvin Harada (Bishop, Buddhist Churches of America – Japanese Pure Land tradition); Rev. Ajahnmaha Prasert (Theravada – Thai tradition); Rev. Hozan Alan Senauke (Berkeley Zen Center – Zen tradition); and Rev. Dr. Heng Sure (Dharma Realm Buddhist Association – Chinese tradition).

I am indebted to Patricia Ikeda-Nash, a colleague and a trusted copy editor, for her superb editing of the manuscript of this book. A big "thank you" goes to my daughter, Serena Tamura, who took time from her demanding schedule as a Ph.D. student to support her father with editing, helping to bridge the age gap with the young readers of this book. My deep appreciation also goes to Ken Nakamura for his numerous suggestions based on his life-long career as a Dharma School teacher and a Scoutmaster. Gratitude is also owed to Jon Murakami of Hawaii for his cartoons and to Rev. Ken Sugahara, the head priest of Gonnenji Temple in Tokyo for his contribution with the graphics.

Also, I feel an enormous sense of gratitude to The Rev. Gyodo Kono Memorial Scholarship Fund at the Midwest Buddhist Temple in Chicago and its selection committee for supporting me again as they have done with my previous publication projects. I am quite confident that their trust in this project will bear fruit in keeping with their mission of informing the wider public about Buddhism.

A Book for the Canadian Audience

This book builds on the book, *Jewels: An Introduction to American Buddhism for Youth, Scouts, and the Young at Heart*, published in in the United States in 2020. In visiting Canada for talks on Buddhism on a number of occasions especially since 2014, I felt a strong wish to produce one for my Canadian friends, who welcomed me and were graciously interested in what I had to share with them.

To realize this goal, I asked two Canadian colleagues to offer their expertise and experiences of Buddhism in Canada. As a result, I am extremely pleased to have Durgesh Kasbekar and John Negru contribute to this book by writing chapters specific to Canadian experience: Chapters 1 and 5 (Durgesh) and 2 (John). Their background information can be found in their bios at the end of the book. Their contributions have made this book worthy of its title, *GEMS: An Introduction to Canadian Buddhism for Young People and the Young at Heart.*

Introduction

THE TITLE OF THIS BOOK, *Gems*, comes from the Buddhist teaching that sees all living beings as precious gems. Each shining gem is located where strands of interconnection cross one another in the vast web of the universe.

You and I, along with all beings, are like the gems that are linked together to illuminate and reflect each other. So as one of the gems in the net, I am connected to the millions of *outer* gems that support and illuminate me.

Also, there lies within each one of us an *inner* gem. It is waiting to shine forth to help us realize Awakening, the aim of Buddhism. In so doing, we will be able to lessen our suffering (sadness, pain, anxiety, etc.) and to realize greater happiness (joy, satisfaction, peace of mind, gratitude, etc.) in this life.[2]

So, the gems symbolize the outer and the inner dimensions or conditions of our lives. Let us first look at the *outer* gems.

Outer Gems

The *outer* gems are talked about in a well-known metaphor called "Indra's Net of Gems" in a scripture called the *Flower Garland Sutra* and related writings.[3] I have expanded on the original version to make it more meaningful to young readers.

An expansive net extends endlessly throughout the universe in all four directions. At each "eye" of the net (where the warp and weft cross) hangs a shining gem. Hence, countless gems are found on the net and together form a galactic bed of shimmering gems. It's an *amazing* sight to behold!

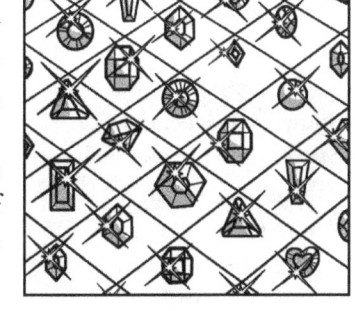

---

[2] "Suffering" is the main English translation of the Sanskrit word *duhkha*. In this book, suffering refers to "sadness, pain, anxiety, disappointment, worries, etc." "Happiness" (*suhkha* in Sanskrit) refers to the absence of suffering and the presence of Awakening, which fosters greater joy, satisfaction, peace of mind, gratitude, etc.

[3] This metaphor continued to be valued in China within the Huayan school of Buddhism and is now often cited by Buddhists in America and beyond.

Since each gem is tied to the net, it is connected to all the other gems. No gem is left out. Each gem feels especially connected to those gems located nearby, for they are easily seen. However, a gem is actually *connected* even to those unseen gems located thousands or even billions of miles away.

Now, no gem can shine by itself. It needs the light from the other gems to shine. This relationship among the gems is called "All for one," for all the other gems are involved in illuminating that one gem.

On the other hand, a gem does not just receive light but also gives out light to illuminate the other gems. Each gem illuminates the nearby gems with greater intensity but also illuminates those gems located thousands of miles away no matter how faint the light might look. This relationship is called "One for all," for that one gem is actively involved in illuminating all the other gems.

Hence, each gem receives light in the "All for one" relationship and simultaneously sends out light in the "One for all" interaction. The gems engage each other in a passive as well as in an active manner. They need each other and help each other. So, the gems are mutually linked, interconnected, and interdependent.

The next important quality of the gems is that each gem is *unique*. Despite the countless number of gems, no two are exactly the same. Every gem is unique in its shape, size, colour and texture. Some are diamond-shaped, some are round or rectangular, and the rest are in every conceivable shape imaginable. The same goes for their size, colour and texture. Some are small as a dewdrop, others as large as a baseball, and others are in between. The colours of some are the primary colours, red, green, and blue, while others are the secondary colours, yellow, magenta and cyan, and others are colours of various mixtures of primary and secondary. The textures vary from smooth to bumpy to jagged to everything in between and beyond. Even the light in each gem differs in colour, sheen and brightness.

So, based on this metaphor, each of us is one of these gems. We are unique, yet dependent on others. We are dependent on others yet can have influence on others. Such is the nature of our existence and our relationship with others, which includes our family, our friends, our community, the nation, the international community, and the natural world.

Yes, the importance of each gem is acknowledged for its unique qualities and for its contribution to others. However, that is not all. Each gem is also valued simply for *existing*. It has worth and value simply for existing and for being a part of this net of gems.

Thus, the Buddhist teachings are ready to help each of us to come to fully realize and appreciate this reality as described by the metaphor and to contribute to greater happiness and peace for others and for ourselves. I believe this offers an *encouraging* and *positive* vision, inspiring us to face up to our problems and to live our lives to the fullest.

Inner Gems

Let us now take a look at the *inner* gems as told in a parable found in another scripture called the *Lotus Sutra*. A poor young man visited the house of a close, rich friend. The friend wined and dined him with delicious food. The poor man had gotten drunk, and he fell asleep. The rich friend had to go out on official business, but before leaving, the rich friend sewed a priceless gem into the lining of his friend's clothes. Not noticing anything, the poor man woke up and set out on a journey to other countries.

The poor young man did not make himself aim for a better life. So, he earned little money and had to be satisfied with very little. It was a struggle to make ends meet. One day, by chance, he ran into his rich friend, who saw how hard life continued to be for his friend. The rich man told the poor friend that there was a priceless gem that had been in his clothing all along. In realizing that he was in possession of a priceless gem, the poor man was overjoyed, for he was now rich enough to try to fulfill his dreams.

The priceless gem that the poor man discovered is a symbol not necessarily of material but of *mental* and *spiritual* happiness. It symbolizes the potentiality that we all have to become a happier, wiser, and better person like the Buddha, the Awakened One. Everyone has the gem within. So unlike in the story where the poor man failed to look within, we should now want to discover that precious gem *on our own*. Let us grab it, polish it and let it shine forth!

Three Gems

"Gems" also make up the Three Gems or Three Treasures, which refer to Buddha (Awakened person), Dharma (the teachings), and Sangha (teachers or community of Buddhists). The Three Gems make up a teaching that all Buddhist schools consider important because it makes up the object of ultimate reliance and respect. A person is considered to have become a "Buddhist" when one accepts the Three Gems as the basic foundation of his or her life. So, "gems" are immensely precious as a teaching and as a metaphor.

I hope that you have gained greater confidence and optimism from the metaphor and the story about the outer and inner gems. It is now up to each of you to *open* your mind and heart to learn the basic teachings and practices.

An "open mind" is like a parachute, for it works best when it's *opened*! So, let us get started.

Part One
Here and Now

1 Buddhism in Canada

Durgesh Kasbekar

Buddhist Population

BUDDHISM IS one of the four major world religions.[4] The other three are Christianity, Islam and Hinduism. These four qualify as "world" religions because they are found in large areas of the world and are not limited to one culture or one corner of the world. There are today 2.3 billion Christians, followed by 1.8 billion Muslims, 1.2 billion Hindus, and 500 million Buddhists. In terms of history, Buddhism is older than Christianity by 500 years and older than Islam by 1,100 years.

Many still perceive Buddhism only as an ancient religion of Asia. However, this view is changing. Buddhists now make up about 1.12 percent of the Canadian population. Out of a total Canadian population of 32,852,320, approximately 366,830 are Buddhists.[5] The Buddhist population in Canada in 1901 was only 10,407.[6] This shows a phenomenal growth of around 35.25 times increase in 110 years. So, Buddhism is one of the fastest growing religions in Canada.

During the period between 2011 and 2018, the number of Christians decreased from 67.3 percent of the Canadian population to 55 percent.[7] Despite the decrease, Christianity is still the largest religion at about 55 percent

---

4. While Christians are still the largest religious group by far, the total percentage of non-Christians (Jews, Buddhists, Muslims, Hindus, and Sikhs.) has increased to 8 percent of the entire Canadian population. Interestingly, there is now a growing number of people who are not part of any religion. In 1971, they accounted for just 4% of the Canadian population which rose to 16.5% (2001), 23.9 % (2011) and 29 % (2018). This does not mean that they are not religious or do not believe in God, but simply are not *affiliated* or go regularly to a church, synagogue, temple, mosque, or any religious organization.

5. Statistics Canada, National Household Survey 2011 https://www150.statcan.gc.ca/n1/pub/91-003-x/2014001/section03/33-eng.htm

6. Suwanda Sugunasiri (2017). Buddhism in Canada – an Oral History. https://tspace.library.utoronto.ca/bitstream/1807/78778/1/Buddhism%20in%20Canada%20%20an%20Oral%20History%20May%202017.pdf

7. Pew Research Center. 2018 five facts about religion in Canada. https://www.pewresearch.org/fact-tank/2019/07/01/5-facts-about-religion-in-canada/

of the population. It is followed by Islam with about 3.2 percent who are Muslims. Next come the Hindus at 1.5 percent and the Sikhs at 1.4 percent. The Buddhists follow at 1.1 percent and, therefore, are slightly more than the Jewish population at 1 percent of the population.

Returning to Buddhism, there are those who do not claim to be "Buddhist" but are keenly interested in the teachings and are engaged in Buddhist practices, especially meditation. They are called "sympathizers" or, sometimes, humourously referred to as "Nightstand Buddhists."[8] They often attend more than one Buddhist temple or centre mostly for meditation sessions or lectures. They practice Buddhism in the privacy of their homes by meditating and reading Buddhist books. After reading Buddhist books in the evening, they place their books on their nightstand, hence, the name, "Nightstand Buddhists." There is no reliable data on the number of "Nightstand Buddhists" in Canada, but their numbers are estimated to be about 2 million in the U.S.[9]

There is another group of people who have been strongly influenced by Buddhism. A survey of Americans revealed that 12 percent of the respondents replied that Buddhism has had an "important influence on their thinking about religion or spirituality."[10] This amounted to a surprisingly large number of about 25 million people in the U.S.[11]

Thus, if we add up all three groups (Buddhists, Nightstand Buddhists, and those influenced by Buddhism), they amount to over 30 million people or about 10 percent of the American population, whose lives have been touched by Buddhism. This indicates how much Buddhism has grown in the past fifty years to become not just a religion of Asia but also an *American* religion.

Drawing parallels from the U.S. figure above, it would be safe to arrive at a conservative figure of around eight percent for Canada for the total number of people who are Buddhists, Nightstand Buddhists, and those influenced by Buddhism. Hence, these three groups would total up to about three million out of the current total Canadian population of approximately 38 million.[12]

---

8. This term was coined by Professor Thomas A. Tweed, a scholar of American religion.

9. Based on the Wuthnow and Cage survey (see below) and the fact that half of the paid subscribers to the Buddhist magazine *Tricycle: The Buddhist Review* do not consider themselves to be Buddhists but are interested enough to read and pay for the magazine.

10. Robert Wuthnow and Wendy Cage, "Buddhists and Buddhism in the United States: The Scope of Influence," *Journal of the Scientific Study of Religion*, Vol. 43, No. 3 (September, 2004):371.

11. This number is based on the year 2003 when the above survey was taken.

12. Canada's population clock (real time model). https://www150.statcan.gc.ca/n1/

There is another factor worth exploring when we look at growth of Buddhism in Canada. As per the National Household Survey of 2011, South Asians (1.6 Million) and Chinese (1.3 million) were the two largest visible minority groups in the country.[13] These two groups are projected to be the two largest minority groups in 2031. South Asians are projected at 3.6 million and the Chinese at 2.7 million.[14] Immigrant Buddhists from Sri Lanka, China, Bhutan, Taiwan and Nepal[15] will form a significant segment of the South Asian and Chinese minority groups.

Various Kinds of Buddhism

What would be your answer if someone asks you, "Which metropolitan area in the world has the largest number of Buddhist *schools* or *denominations*?" Most people probably would answer, "Bangkok, Taipei or Kyoto" because they still see Buddhism as a religion of Asia.

Yes, it's true that the vast majority of the approximately 500 million Buddhists in the world live in Asia. However, here the question has to do with the number of different *schools* or *denominations*, not population. Surprisingly, the answer to that question would be Los Angeles, California metropolitan area, where close to 100 different schools of Buddhism find their home. In other words, virtually all the main schools or denominations of Buddhism in Asia are now represented in Los Angeles.

However, Toronto and Vancouver follow close behind Los Angeles. In Toronto and Vancouver, numerous temples with roots in China, Japan, Thailand, Korea, Laos, Cambodia, and Vietnam are in the same town or even on the same street.

Of the 1.2 million people of Chinese descent who had chosen to reside in Canada by 2006, Toronto and Vancouver received a disproportionately high number of residents. By 2006, Toronto's Chinese Canadian population numbered 486,330, while in Vancouver, the number was 381,535, which means that a majority chose Toronto and Vancouver over other cities. Per the 2016 Census, the number of Canadians of Chinese origin had risen to

---

pub/71-607-x/71-607-x2018005-eng.htm

13. Canadian demographics at a glance. Statistics Canada. https://www150.statcan.gc.ca/n1/pub/91-003-x/2014001/section03/32-eng.htm

14. Please see above.

15. The Buddhist population of Nepal is about 9% of its total population. Source: Population monograph of Nepal Volume II Social Demography. https://nepal.unfpa.org/sites/default/files/pub-pdf/Population%20Monograph%20V02.pdf

1.8 million.[16, 17]

In 1960, there were fewer than 25 Buddhist organizations in Canada. By 2021, there were 619 Buddhist temples, centres, associations, groups, and resources within communities in just about every major city in the ten provinces and three territories.[18] Statistics Canada shows the presence of Buddhists even in the Northwestern territories close to the Arctic.[19]

Table[20, 21] - Buddhist organizations[22] in different provinces

Provinces	Organizations
Ontario	243
British Columbia	163
Quebec	73
Alberta	68
Nova Scotia	35
Saskatchewan	12
Manitoba	11
New Brunswick	5
Newfoundland & Labrador	3
Prince Edward Island	3
Yukon	2
Nunavut	1
Northwest Territories	0
Total	619

---

16. Chinese Canadians (n.d.). https://www.thecanadianencyclopedia.ca/en/article/chinese-canadians

17. We would like to qualify that not all Chinese would be of Buddhist faith. Many among them would belong to Christian denominations as well.

18. Negru, John Harvey, "Highlights from the survey of Canadian Buddhist Organizations," *Journal of Global Buddhism* Vol. 14(2013): 1-18

19. Please see Suganasiri above.

20. The Sumeru guide to Canadian Buddhism (n.d.). http://www.directory.sumeru-books.com/about-2/history/

21. The Sumeru Directory website is hosted by Canadian Buddhist scholar John Harvey Negru (Karma Yönten Gyatso), who has put in more than ten years in maintaining a database of Canadian Buddhist organizations. The list was last revised in March 2022.

22. Includes temples, centres, meditation groups, charities, associations and blogs.

To enhance the understanding of all the various kinds of Buddhist schools, we have categorized them into four groups. They are as follows:

Older Asian Canadian Buddhists. They started their temples in late 1800s and are mostly of Chinese and Japanese origin. Currently as there are more third, fourth and fifth generation Canadians, their temple activities and services are held in English.

Newer Asian Canadian Buddhists. They mostly arrived in Canada since the mid-1960s and are mostly of Chinese, Cambodian, Korean, Laotian, Myanmarese, Sri Lankan, Taiwanese, Thai, and Vietnamese origin. With a large percentage of first-generation members, the temple activities and services are often held in native languages. However, English is increasingly used as the second and third generations come of age.

Convert Buddhists whose main practice is meditation. Unlike the first two groups, they were not born into Buddhist families but have converted to Buddhism as adults. They are predominately European Canadians and belong to one of the three schools, Zen, Vipassana (meaning "insight," based on the Theravada tradition of Southeast Asia) or Tibetan. Their main practice is sitting meditation. The immense popularity of mindfulness (insight) meditation has increased their numbers especially as we entered the 21st century.

Some famous Canadian Buddhists can be categorized within this group. They include the late singer, song writer and poet Leonard Cohen, internationally published author Albert Low (also deceased), a well-known hockey coach Jim Bedard, singer songwriters Alanis Morissette and k.d. Lang, and actor Jim Carey.[23] They reflect Canada's contemporary society and represent a wide range of professions that encompass literary artists, performing artists, and sports personnel. The 2nd chapter of this book authored by John Negru provides a detailed list of famous Canadian Buddhists.

Convert Buddhists whose main practice is chanting. Converts to Buddhism as adults, they belong to one school, Soka Gakkai International– Canada. They are racially the *most diverse* group for they include Canadians of Asian, European, African, and Hispanic origin. Their main practice is the repeated chanting of the name of the *Lotus Sutra* or the "*daimoku,*" which is pronounced "*Nam-myōhō-renge-kyō.*"

---

23. Celebrity Buddhists. A blog by Tsem Rinpoche. https://www.tsemrinpoche.com/tsem-tulku-rinpoche/current-affairs/celebrity-buddhists.html

These four groups are a part of many other sets of classification created by scholars to identify various kinds of Buddhists. One such classification includes two groups, "Acquired Buddhists (AB)" and "Inherited Buddhists (IB)" as proposed by Canadian Buddhist scholar Suwanda Sugunasiri.[24]

The Acquired Buddhists are first-generation Buddhists. They did not grow up Buddhist. They grew up in families that were of other religions, usually Christian or Jewish, or of no religion. However, they came to embrace Buddhism when they reached adulthood by leaving behind their religion.

On the other hand, Inherited Buddhists are those who grew up in Buddhist families and continue to be Buddhists as adults. Most of these Inherited Buddhists correspond to groups one and two in the above category, the Older Asian-Canadian Buddhists, and the Newer Asian-Canadian Buddhists.

Characteristics of Buddhism in Canada

Buddhism in North America has developed characteristics that differ from those in traditional Asian Buddhist countries. This trend is especially strong in the convert Buddhist communities, groups 3 and 4 in the first classification and the Acquired Buddhists of the second classification discussed above. These characteristics are 1) equality 2) practice-focused 3) scientific 4) socially engaged and 5) here and now.

Equality. This equality is related to gender as well as to the relationship between the clergy and the lay people. Women play an equal role in Canada compared to Asia. There are more women teachers in proportion to men than their counterparts in Asian countries. Regarding the clergy, monks and nuns are the norm in virtually all of the Buddhist countries in Asia, but Canadian Buddhists have largely rejected the monastic lifestyle of the monks and nuns. Thus, most Canadian clergy or priests are married with families. Further, the lay people play a much stronger role in temples and centres, especially in matters related to the management of the institutions. These democratic developments of equality differ from the more traditional hierarchical relationships in Asia, where monks and nuns are considered superior to laypeople, and men are considered superior to women.

Practice-focused. When people belonging to many denominations come together for a Buddhist gathering, they tend to ask each other, "What's your practice?" rather than "What's your denomination or school?" This is

---

24. Sugunasiri also proposes the duality of "Ethnic-Buddhists" and "Euro-Buddhists". (Crowe, 2014)

because Canadian Buddhists value practice, which comes mostly in the form of meditation and chanting. Such Buddhist practices are popular, as we saw above, among the third and fourth groups above.

More Canadians seek to *experience* their religion with their total being by going beyond just knowing the teachings in their heads. Some of them may feel that the religion in which they grew up had plenty of creeds to live by and doctrines to memorize, but satisfaction and fulfillment was elusive. But *meditation* makes them feel more relaxed, focused and liberated. In other words, meditation is therapeutic and empowering, while providing them with the sense that they are working toward spiritual awakening.

In addition, anyone interested can practice these meditations anytime and anywhere. In Asia, mostly monks and nuns practice meditation in a formal setting in the presence of a teacher. It is also rare for men and women to meditate in the same room together. However, in Canada with some initial instructions, people are able to practice by themselves, even in the privacy of their home and at any time that suits them.

One of the most popular forms of meditation, called "mindfulness meditation," is also popular in Canada. Mindfulness meditation is the same technique as Buddhist vipassana, or insight meditation. Currently, young and old are practicing mindfulness meditation in schools, prisons, hospitals and workplaces. It has been reported that some children and youth become more calm and focused on their schoolwork if they learn how to do mindfulness meditation. (See p. 93)

As a result, many people no longer consider mindfulness a "religious" practice because it has been separated from its Buddhist roots. Some Buddhists are alarmed and unhappy about this trend, but this should be seen as another characteristic of how Buddhism has been adapted in Canada.

Scientific. Psychology (which includes psychotherapy) has become one of the avenues for Canadians to become interested in and to understand Buddhism, since they both focus on the mind and seek to overcome suffering. Consequently, many counselors and therapists have converted to Buddhism or adopted Buddhist elements such as meditation into their professional practices.

Another reason for the popularity of Buddhism is that it does not conflict with natural science. This view contributed to the popularity of Fritjof Capra's landmark book *The Tao of Physics*, published in 1975.

The Dalai Lama, the world-famous Buddhist leader, has been at the forefront of dialogue between Buddhists and scientists. In fact, he has gone so far as to announce that in the area of the natural world, if there is any conflict with science, Buddhists should adjust their traditional understanding in accordance with science. This does nothing in proving Buddhist teachings false or irrelevant. For example, Buddhists can adopt Charles Darwin's theory of evolution without any problem, for the view that we humans evolved from so-called lesser life forms does nothing to make the Buddhist teachings false or irrelevant.

Socially Engaged. Many Canadian Buddhists believe that Buddhism must help to lessen the problems of the world, such as global warming, domestic violence, poverty, discrimination, and crime. Their view is that Buddhism should not only be concerned with one's own happiness but should also care about others, especially those who are suffering.

This is not to say social engagement is absent in Asia, for example, as will be discussed later, King Ashoka of India built medical clinics and made traveling easier. (See p. 51) Priests and their supporters helped to build bridges and irrigation ponds, while others ran temples that served as community centres where people gathered for advice on everyday life problems. So, we believe that for centuries before the modern period, the level of social engagement for Buddhists in Asia and Christians in the West was basically the same.

However, Buddhism in Canada began its journey in late 19th century as a "modern" religion, when people felt that religions should contribute even more actively to make the world a better place. This thought has influenced many Canadian Buddhists – past and present. This outlook about religion and its role in society has no doubt been strengthened by Jewish and Christian traditions of *social justice* that are prominent in Canadian culture.

"Here and now." In Asia, the traditional teachings regarded our present life as lying within the cycle of innumerable births and deaths (*samsara*), which is often translated as "reincarnation" or "transmigration." The ideal Buddhist way of life was to "leave the world" to become a monk or a nun to focus on the Buddhist goal of spiritual Awakening (*nirvana*). By accomplishing that, they believed that they could be freed from the endless cycles of transmigration which a person experienced through births and deaths.

It would be like getting on a Ferris wheel. The first few rounds are fun and interesting, but it would be boring and dreadful if you had to go around and around cooped up in the same capsule and seeing the same scenery endlessly. Hence, for monks and nuns, the present life was an opportunity for learning and practice so as to reach Awakening to "transcend" the endless cycle of births and deaths.

In contrast to Asia, a miniscule number of Canadian Buddhists become monks and nuns. The vast majority of Buddhist teachers are householders and lead ordinary lives in the world. They do not make it their primary aim to be liberated from transmigration but, instead, actively seek Awakening in this present life and body.

For example, the important Buddhist teaching, "everything changes" (*anitya*), is not understood by most Canadian Buddhists as a reason for *not* getting *attached* to things, as it would be for monks and nuns. Rather, this teaching is taken as an encouragement to live fully "in the moment" and is reflected in a popular saying quoted by Buddhists:

> Yesterday is history and tomorrow is a mystery. But this moment is a gift, and that is why we call it the *present!*

We love this quotation, which expresses the outlook that the Buddha himself expressed. (See p. 108)

Reasons for the Popularity of Buddhism

When something becomes popular, we can look at it from the standpoint of "supply" and "demand." This is true for a product (for example, a video game), or sports (soccer), or certain values (protecting the environment). The popularity of Buddhism in Canada should be seen in the same light.

The "supply" side of Buddhism refers to the qualities that many Canadians see and like about Buddhism. And those qualities are the very characteristics that were described in the previous section, "The Characteristics of Buddhism in Canada." In other words, many Canadians see in Buddhism a religion (or spirituality or philosophy) that *supplies* them with the qualities of equality, practice-focus, scientific outlook, and here-and-now.

As we have discussed these qualities in detail, we would now like to look at the "demand" side. This refers to those factors that "pull" and "welcome" Buddhism to Canada. These factors are 1) the importance of religion for Canadians; 2) the historical changes that made Canadian society more open; 3) the changes in what people seek in religion; and 4) the popularity of the Dalai Lama and Thich Nhat Hanh.

The importance of religion. Though maybe slightly less than Americans, Canadians do value religion. They generally hold pastors, priests, rabbis, and religious professionals in high regard. Moreover, many of these religious leaders play important roles as leaders of the *general* community over and beyond their churches, temples, mosques, and synagogues.

Religion is seen to be "a good thing," providing a spiritual and ethical foundation especially for children. This is why many parents take their children to church in the belief that religion will help them to be happy and ethical when they grow up.

Many of us take this positive view of religion for granted, but this is not necessarily true in other developed societies in the world, including Japan and France.[25] Religion plays a *less* important role in the lives of people living in those countries. This can be attributed to a process called "secularism."[26] So, if religion were not as important in Canada, far fewer people would be taking interest in Buddhism.

Societal openness. The second reason for the growth of Buddhism in Canada lies in the fundamental societal shift that took place in the 1960s, with greater openness toward religions other than Protestantism. For example, John F. Kennedy became the first Catholic president of the United States, which did have some impact on Canada. The Catholic Church itself became more open to change in its teachings, rituals, and relationship with other religions in a liberalization process initiated by the "Second Vatican Council."

Greater Diversity. The new Canadian immigration Act of 1967 did away all the restrictive and racially prejudiced immigration legislations of yester years and heralded a new era in Canadian immigration. It helped to foster greater diversity with the arrival of more people from non-Western countries, including those in Asia. Canada also has a distinct strength in nurturing pluralism and diversity. It enacted the Canadian Multiculturalism Act, 1988 that aims to enhance ethnic and cultural diversity across the country.

Changes to Buddhist Population[27]

Year	Population	% Increase
1981	51,955	-
1991	163,415	+214.5%
2001	300,345	+ 83.8%
2011	366,830	+ 22.1%

Within this greater openness, Buddhism was no longer seen as an exotic

---

25. We wish to qualify that people in these countries do value the essence of religion but do not take their children on a regular basis to temples and churches for religious education.

26. As secularism becomes stronger, religion becomes less important for people and society.

27. Please see Sugunasiri, page 4.

religion of the Orient. In fact, many people interested in spiritual matters thought that "spiritual Asia" was superior to "materialistic West." Consequently, many people were attracted to Buddhism because they thought Buddhism was one of the "superior" Asian religions that could respond better to the spiritual needs of the industrialized West.

4) Spirituality. The third reason for this growth has to do with the change in the very nature of religion in Canada. In this change, people have become more attracted to spirituality than organized religion, such as churches, synagogues, temples and mosques. More people are heard saying, "I am not religious but spiritual."

A famous scholar of religion explained spirituality as "personal experience tailored to the individual's own quests." He then went on to define "spirituality" in five key terms: *connectedness, unity, peace, harmony,* and *centredness*. This differs from the five terms that characterize traditional religion, which are *God, sin, faith, repentance,* and *morals*.[28]

Buddhism, as seen in Canada, is characterized more by the former set of terms than the latter, which makes it fit more with the changing or new trend centred on spirituality. As part of this attraction to spirituality that stresses personal experience, Buddhism has been particularly effective in the following three areas.

The first is the healthy attitude of Buddhism when dealing with the suffering from the difficulties we face in life, such as old age, death, and loss. Buddhism sees difficulties as a *natural* part of life that needs to be understood, accepted, and turned into a springboard for living a more full and meaningful life.

Second, Buddhism has been valuable in the *personal* understanding of many individuals, because the Buddhist teachings need to speak directly to the experience of unique individuals. Many Canadians like to feel they are free to question religious teachings and to make up their own minds about them. This is the reason why many Canadian Buddhists, along the lines of American Buddhists, are fond of these famous words of the Buddha: "Do not accept a statement on the grounds that it is found in our scriptures...or because it's the authority of the teachers"[29]

The third area of spirituality is found in people's attraction to meditation. This is probably the number one reason for the growth of Buddhism in Canada. Many find Buddhist meditation easy to do, mentally therapeutic, and spiritually empowering and liberating. Sitting meditation, in

---

28. Wade Clark Roof, "Religious Kaleidoscope," *Temenos* 32 (1996):183–193.

29. Lama Surya Das, *Awakening the Buddha Within*, (Broadway Books, 1998), p. 388. Quoted by Das to show what Americans like about Buddhism.

particular, is the main practice in Zen, Theravada, and Tibetan schools, which have attracted a high number of converts.

5) The popularity of the Dalai Lama and Thich Nhat Hanh. The fourth reason for the growth lies in the positive image of two individuals, the fourteenth Dalai Lama, Tenzin Gyatso and Thich Nhat Hanh. The Dalai Lama is a renowned Nobel Peace Prize laureate and exiled leader of Tibet. His impact in the West has been enormous. He is loved and held in esteem by thousands who flock to hear his talks during his Canadian visits. He is popular because people see him as a spiritual leader who is peaceful, tolerant, and friendly. He has helped to foster a new and refreshing image of a religious leader in North America.

The same can be said of the late Thich Nhat Hanh, the Paris-based Vietnamese Buddhist monk who passed away in January 2022. In terms of influence of Buddhist leaders in the West, he ranks second only to the Dalai Lama. He inspired Dr. Martin Luther King Jr. and others to oppose the Vietnam War, which resulted in Dr. King nominating him to the Nobel Peace prize in 1967. Famous for his 1975 book *The Miracle of Mindfulness*, he visited Canada twice and is popular in Canadian populace going beyond the Canadian Vietnamese Buddhist community.

So, Buddhism has become very much part of the Canadian landscape. Buddhist places of worship are no longer anomalies or novelties but have become integral and accepted part of most Canadian towns.

Where did all of this begin? To understand the answer to this question, we need to go back around 2,600 years, to the foothills of the Himalayas, and to learn more about the birth of a man whom the Buddhists call "the Buddha."

We will look at that beginning in the third chapter.

2 Living Buddhist Experiences in Canada

John Negru

THERE MAY BE no such thing as Canadian Buddhism, but there is plenty of Buddhist practice in Canada. There are more than 550 Buddhist organizations here. You can find them in most Canadian cities and towns. There are rural retreat centres too. From the BC Channel Islands to the coast of Cape Breton NS, in St. John's NL or Whitehorse YK, there are folks invoking Buddhist energy on the path to Enlightenment and a more enlightened, sustainable society right at this moment.

Some have deeper roots in Canada than others, but there is a joyful diversity of traditions, lineages, cultural treasures, and deep reflection here, to experience and grow within. You can see that splendid array simply by visiting the canadianbuddhism.info directory of Canadian Buddhist organizations. Virtually every lineage and tradition is represented in our country!

As you read this book, there are some things we know for sure and much we don't know. There are also some things that are forever mysterious and miraculous.

We know that while Buddhist practice has been around for almost 150 years in Canada, the number of Canadians who identify as Buddhist expanded exponentially in the past 50 years. as discussed in Chapter 1. Buddhist thought has also permeated many aspects of our culture, so it is no longer something foreign and exotic.

Many thousands of your fellow Canadian citizens have worked tirelessly to be good Buddhist ancestors to you and your children yet to be born. They have built temples, retreat centres and charities, endowed university programmes, and much more, to share the refuge of the Three Gems (Buddha, Teachings and Community) in a way that is in tune with nature and social justice. They have devoted countless hours to meditation, cultivation of the Way, and service to others. Their example is profoundly admirable.

We know the future is going to be very different from the recent past and even the present. Many challenges await us, and the world is full of shallow distractions. Tomorrow's leaders will need virtues such as clear-headedness, compassion, consensus-building, cooperation, and commitment to transparency. These are not skills easily learned. In the future, Enlightenment will need to be crowdsourced.

In sailing, there is a tool called a kedge, used in stormy seas to keep a ship on course. Several sailors row out ahead of the main ship and drop an anchor (the kedge). The ship then uses that kedge to haul itself forward to where it needs to be. Buddhist practice is rather like that kedge. It's an anchor pulling us forward while we navigate turbulent waters.

We know there are now many more Buddhist books, movies, websites, university programmes, and so on than there ever were before. Admittedly, it can get a bit confusing. Direct experience has always been highly prized in Buddhist practice, but that doesn't mean you can't or shouldn't search out whatever Buddhist resources speak to you. Shakyamuni Buddha famously said, essentially, "Don't take my word for it on faith. Weigh what I'm saying and if it makes sense try it out. Then evaluate whether it has been beneficial for you and those around you." Your authentic curiosity and openness are your passport to that expanded vision of life and reality. Identifying as Buddhist is much less important than practicing Buddhism!

I'm writing this chapter as a Buddhist activist with more than 50 years of community development experience, founder of Canada's largest Buddhist book publishing company and host of the canadianbuddhism.info directory. I've been remarkably blessed to learn from many teachers and to have shared the journey with a fascinating group of Dharma friends. But for these past few years, I've been reflecting more and more on the future: on you.

Back in 2012, when I conducted Canada's first national sociological survey of Buddhist organizations, in cooperation with the Department of Religious Studies at the University of Toronto, one of the important issues that came from the data was that Buddhism in Canada skews heavily towards older Canadians, and many Buddhist organizations seemed unprepared or at a loss as to how to convey the treasures of Buddhist practice to the next generation.

The challenges of today seem vastly different from those of an earlier Age. On one hand, we are awakening to our Anthropocene overshoot crisis, with humans taking more than the planet can sustain, leading to climate crises, extinctions and other challenges. On the other hand, Covid-19 has shown us how fragile our situation really is. These wake-up calls have brought humanity's possible future trajectories into sharp focus and how our decisions will determine the outcome for Earth and all its inhabitants.

Perhaps in an older version of Buddhism, practice was all about what happened on the meditation cushion. In the Buddhism of the future, it is all about what you do when you get up again from the cushion. It is serious business, as any Zen kōan will tell you.

Shakyamuni said: "Ehipassiko," loosely translated as "come and see for yourself."

I can't tell you what it was like to be born into a Buddhist family. When I discovered Buddhism in the 1960s, I was looking for a philosophy that offered broader vistas than the Judeo-Christian visions of Montreal, where I grew up as a nice, middle class Jewish boy down the street from Leonard Cohen, who would go on to become a world-famous songwriter and poster child for Zen Buddhism. Our mothers were occasional tea buddies. Québec was in the midst of the Quiet Revolution of secularization, and the Beatles were preaching the merits of Eastern religion.

Of course, there are famous Canadian Buddhists. His Holiness the Dalai Lama is one of only a handful of Honorary Canadian citizens. Leonard Cohen spent years in rigourous Zen practice. k.d. lang is well-known for her Buddhist, vegan and LGBTQI commitment. But there are so many others who have immersed themselves in practice and teaching here in Canada. They may only be leaders within their own communities, or devoted community members whose efforts are not widely recognized in mainstream media, but they are definitely the pulsing energy of what we could call Canadian Buddhism.

They're devoting their time to helping out at the foodbank or Kids Help Phone, creating mandalas from sand for world peace at the Canadian National Exhibition, sitting in stillness in a mountain cabin, studying and teaching the legacy of those gone before, chanting powerful mantras of transformation, invoking the energy of the Buddhas, Bodhisattvas and Arhats to cultivate more Enlightened thought, speech and action, and so on. These days, you're as likely to see Buddhists at a climate demonstration as you are to see Buddhists in robes burning incense in front of a Buddha statue. And that's a good thing.

So here's a shout out to some of those folks, in no particular order...

Give these folks a big shout-out!

Sean Hillman, former Buddhist monk, medical ethicist in a Toronto hospital network and volunteer chaplain in the Canadian prison system. Also, an awesome heavy metal drummer!

Chris Ng, tireless community organizer who has been integral to the development of the University of Toronto's Buddhism, Psychology and Mental Health programme, their Buddhist Chaplaincy programme, and a variety of other organizations such as the Buddhist Education Foundation for Canada, and the Toronto Centre for Applied Buddhism.

Tynette Deveaux, long-time editor of *Lion's Roar* Buddhist magazine in Halifax, who in 2021 left to become the communications director for Sierra Club Canada's Beyond Coal campaign in Atlantic Canada.

Glenn Mullin, from the Gaspé, fluent in Tibetan, citizen of the world, known for his books on Vajrayana Buddhism and his workshops everywhere from Mongolia to Korea, Russia, the United States and beyond.

Richard Bryan McDaniel, the leading historian of all things Zen Buddhist in North America, based in Fredericton, New Brunswick. He's also the creator of the YMCA Peace Medallion, by the way.

Tanya McGinnity, long-time Buddhist blogger in Montreal, who recently passed 250 conversations for Kids Help Phone as a crisis responder. She also edited *Lotus Petals in the Snow: Voices of Canadian Buddhist Women*, an anthology of more than 25 contributions from across Canada.

The late Professor Herbert Guenther, of Saskatoon, whose meticulous translations of ancient Buddhist texts in the 1960s were fundamental to the growth of Buddhist Studies in the West.

Geshe Thubten Jinpa, based in Montreal and official translator for His Holiness the Dalai Lama, amongst his many other accomplishments.

Glenn Copeland, New Brunswick's black trans musical treasure, loved around the world – a Soka Gakkai Nichiren devotee.

Ray Innen Parchelo, founding representative of Japan's modern Tendai lineage in Canada, in Renfrew, ON.

Dianne Harke, of Nelson, BC, who wrote a wonderful Young Adult novel about Alexandra David-Neel, one of the world's great explorers a hundred years ago and early expounder of Buddhist teachings for a Western audience.

Professor Paul Keddy, world-renowned wetlands ecologist, supporter of a variety of Nature Conservancy Trusts, and Green Buddhist advocate. He lives in a 100-acre wood near Ottawa that is bequeathed in perpetuity to stay wild.

Bhante Mihita, who was Suwanda Sugunasiri before he ordained in retirement as a monk. Bhante is responsible for the creation of Canada's first pan-Buddhist celebration of Buddha's Birthday (Vesak) in Toronto in 1981. That annual event is now held in Mississauga's Celebration Square, hosted by more than 40 Buddhist temples and attended by thousands of people. Bhante was also the community organizer behind the Buddhist Council of Canada, the Canadian Buddhist Literary Festival, and many other initiatives.

Bhante Saranapala, of the Brampton Buddhist Mission, another tireless community organizer, who now orchestrates Toronto's annual Vesak as well as playing a key role in the nurturing of Buddhist social work initiatives, supporting Brampton's Sri Lankan community, and chaplaincy training at the University of Toronto.

Professor Jessica Main, Chair and Director of the Robert H.N. Ho Family Foundation programme in Buddhism at the University of British Columbia.

Professor Frances Garrett, Director of the Buddhism, Psychology and Mental Health programme at the University of Toronto.

Bhikkhuni Tinh Quang, from Hamilton, who can often be found helping out at the St. Francis Table open kitchen.

Vimalasara, *aka* Valerie Mason-John, the Black Buddhist teacher from British Columbia who is a leader in the field of addiction recovery. Plus, I never get tired of listening to her because she talks just like Adele.

Mr. Lu, who founded a Buddhist temple on Pender Street in Vancouver in 1973 and inaugurated it that summer with the help of Tripitaka Master Hsuan Hua Shih from Gold Mountain Monastery in San Francisco and Kalu Rinpoche from Darjeeling, who was in Canada to establish a Tibetan Buddhist centre in Vancouver. (I was there.)

Rosemary Than, who served as secretary for the Toronto Buddhist Federation and representative for the Burmese Buddhist community, back in the 1980s.

The late Tashi Lhanendapo, who started Canada's first Tibetan handicraft store, on Scollard Street in Toronto back in 1977. I think it was called The Jewel Ornament. He had been a monk back in Tibet and came to Canada in the early 1970s. Canada was one of the first countries to welcome Tibetan refugees and their communities across Canada have become well established, but the largest "Little Tibet" in the country is still the Parkdale neighbourhood in Toronto. The Tibetans who arrived in 1971 where the first non-European refugees invited to Canada. Tashi was a loveable skinny little guy who always seemed a bit agitated, kind of like Kramer on Seinfeld. He died of cancer in 1991 and I miss him. There are quite a few Tibetan handicraft stores now (although the goods are made in Nepal or India by Tibetans in exile).

The late Eileen Swinton, who ran The Snow Lion Tibet Shoppe on Queen Street West and then East in Toronto through the 1980s and 90s.

Linda Hochstetler, social worker, a tireless advocate for education around end-of-life issues. She's also a Buddhist teacher in Toronto. Francine Geraci is another practitioner I know who has done a lot of hospice work in Toronto.

Ajahn Sona, whose Birken Forest Monastery near Kamloops, BC, is a model of environmental sustainability. The Ajahn has shared his expertise with rural Buddhist communities across North America and Europe.

Kuya Minogue, a Zen teacher in Creston, BC, and Bonnie Ryan-Fisher, a mindfulness teacher in Whitecourt, AB, who have each written meditation guides.

Vivian Tsang, student of Master Tam Shek-wing (himself the author of more than 80 books on Buddhism), based in Toronto, translator and editor of Buddhist texts when she's not busy with her career in Artificial Intelligence and educational software for children.

Rod Burylo, an international speaker, business author, media contributor, and consultant specializing in the financial services and accounting industries, who also happens to be a Past President of the Calgary Buddhist Temple and author of a very informative book on personal finance and corporate governance from a Buddhist perspective.

Samu Sunim, who came to Canada in 1969 as a young Korean Zen Buddhist monk. He was the first Buddhist teacher I ever met, in his sparsely furnished apartment on Avenue du Parc in Montreal. Three things I didn't know then were that Samu Sunim would become a great North American Buddhist teacher, that our paths would cross many times, or that he would be a beacon for me even fifty years later. And his lifestyle was still very humble and austere until his passing away in 2022.

Samu Sunim, 2009

Photo courtesy of John Negru

Daryl Lynn Ross, who practiced with me back in the same sangha in the 1970s, became a chaplain at Concordia University in later years, and is one of the founding teachers at True North Insight/Centre de méditation vipassana Voie boréale.

Shirley Johannesen, yoga teacher from Calgary, founder of Sakyadhita International Association of Buddhist Women's Canadian organization.

Venerable Acharya Zasep Tulku Rinpoche in Toronto and then Nelson, BC, the late Geshe Khenrab Gajam in Montreal, and Lama Tsewang Gyurmed in Vancouver, the first ordained Tibetan Buddhist teachers to settle in Canada in the 1970s.

Darshan Chaudry, of the Toronto Buddhist Mahavihara, who was on the Board of the Toronto Buddhist Federation with me in the 1980s. He taught all of us about the amazing social justice work of Dr. Bhimrao Ambedkar, the Indian Buddhist lawmaker who drafted India's Constitution and who worked his entire life for the uplift of India's poorest citizens, the so-called Untouchables (now referred to as the Dalit class). We should all learn more about Dr. Ambedkar and be inspired by his work to end caste discrimination.

Dolma Tulotsang, organizer for the Kalachakra Initiation in Toronto in 2004, conducted for several thousand participants over 10 days, by His Holiness the XIVth Dalai Lama.

Chris Banigan, the Toronto graphic designer who became one of the West's leading Tibetan icon painters.

Ngawang Norbu Kheyap, a famous Tibetan icon painter in his homeland, but invisible to all but his family and close community in his Canadian home in Calgary.

The late Rev. Doreen Hamilton, a Minister at the Toronto Buddhist Church, a former public health nurse and founder of the Mother Goose Parent-Child drop-in programme for new mothers.

Sister Elaine MacInnes, Catholic Nun and Zen Master, from Moncton, NB, but now living in Toronto, and one of the leading lights for Zen practice amongst Catholics. She is a founding director for the Prison Phoenix Trust in the UK. Her work in prison reform is one of the not-mentioned-enough foundation stones of the Civil Rights movement around the world.

Sensei Frank Ulrich, the German-Métis Minister at the Winnipeg Buddhist Church until his retirement in 2014, an interfaith pioneer in so many ways but particularly in building bridges with Winnipeg's Indigenous Communities and welcoming their Elders' wisdom into his practice, teaching and ministry.

I could go on, but you get the idea. There are so many amazing Canadian Buddhists it boggles the mind! After all, like I said before, there are more than 550 Buddhist organizations in Canada.

And Then This Happened

I'm old. You're young. Here's some stuff that happened that you might want to know about. It's not exactly in chronological order, but it might give you some sense of the range and depth of Buddhism in Canada.

The Lytton Chinese History Museum

As if the pandemic were not enough, British Columbia has been stricken with wildfires, the hottest temperature ever recorded in Canada, and floods this past summer. The town of Lytton, where that temperature was reached (49.5°C), burned to the ground in one of those fires and it was all over the news. Here's a story about it that didn't make the news.

One of the destroyed buildings on Main Street housed the Lytton Chinese History Museum.[30] Lytton was home to Canada's first Buddhist temple, dedicated to Kwan Yin, that stood from 1881 to 1928, originally built by Chinese railway workers. Flash forward to now. Lions Gate Buddhist Priory, located just up the valley on the outskirts of town, has been commemorating the original temple with an annual Kwan Yin Festival for peace and healing at the site for quite a few years, including a vegetarian

---

30. https://lyttonchinesehistorymuseum.com/

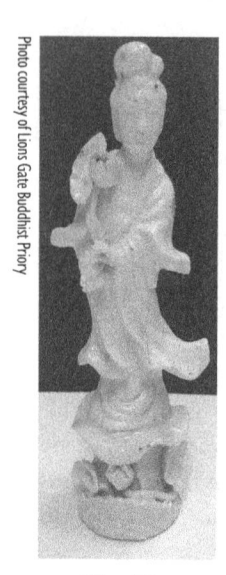

potluck afterwards. The Priory was one of the organizations actively campaigning for more awareness for this piece of history. In 2016, the site was officially recognized as a Chinese Historical Places Site by the BC government. That's how the museum got started. This summer when the town burned, the monks and nuns at Lions Gate Priory were forced to evacuate, but fortunately their property was not destroyed by the fire as well. Like the townsfolk, they were helped by local Indigenous communities. Now they are home and hoping to restore the museum and its artifacts. One of the few items to remain unscathed by the fire was this small porcelain statue of Kwan Yin.

The Black Hat

The Karmapa, head of the Kagyu lineage of Tibetan Buddhism, wears a black hat symbolically linked to that tradition. In the Black Hat Initiation, he takes the black hat out of a case, puts it on his head, and holds it in place with his right hand. It is said that those who attend experience Liberation Through Seeing on the spot. In 1976, the XVIth Karmapa performed that ceremony at the Deer Park United Church on St. Clair Avenue West in Toronto.

The Kalachakra

In 2004, His Holiness the Dalai Lama bestowed the ten-day Kalachakra

(Wheel of Time) Initiation[31] in Toronto for thousands of people. He has visited quite a few times since his first visit in 1977 and is an Honorary Canadian citizen.

The Maitreya Heart Shrine Relic Tour

The Maitreya Heart Shrine Relic Tour came through Canada several times between 2009 and 2011 in its 11 years on the road. The travelling exhibition featured the relics of 42 Buddhist masters, including the 2,600-year-old remains of Buddha himself. It visited 67 countries and drew more than 1.7 million viewers.

Open Heart

In 2011, Thich Nhat Hanh, the late Vietnamese Zen monk and Nobel Peace Prize nominee who is best known for his gentle mindfulness practices and his non-violent social justice work, visited Vancouver to lead a six-day retreat, "Awakening the Heart," followed by a public talk, "Open Mind, Open Heart: Touching the Wonders of Now."

The Jade Buddha for Universal Peace

The Jade Buddha for Universal Peace was sculpted in the image of the Shakyamuni Buddha *rupa* in the Mahabodhi Temple in Bodhgaya. It is carved from a single piece of Polar Pride jade, found in Canada in 2000. It is the largest Buddha statue in the world that is carved from a single piece of gem-quality jade. It is 2.7 metres tall and now resides in Australia, but during the summer of 2010 it visited several Canadian cities on its world tour before arriving at its forever home.

Big Hearts

Buddhist organizations have big hearts. Many temples support schools, orphanages, disaster recovery and food programmes in Asia. Gaden Relief has donated more than $500,000 for projects in India, Tibet, and Mongolia.

---

31. https://www.dalailama.com/teachings/kalachakra-initiations

The Tung Lin Kok Yuen Canada Society in Vancouver has donated millions of dollars to Canadian public institutions, including $10 million to the Lions Gate Hospital in Vancouver in 2011. Tzu Chi Buddhist Compassion Foundation has donated more than $100,000 to Toronto hospitals. These are big numbers, but little temples also do lots. They just don't make the news.

Racism

The story of the internment of Japanese Canadians during World War II is well documented, as is the exclusionism faced by Chinese labourers in Canada. Sadly, some Buddhists in Canada still face ongoing racism. A Sri Lankan temple in Toronto has been firebombed multiple times. A Sri Lankan temple in Ottawa has had the Buddha statue on its lawn smashed multiple times. A large Buddha statue was stolen from an Oakville cemetery. Recently swastikas were spray painted on the doors of a Japanese Buddhist temple in Calgary. Canadian temples have had trouble bringing in qualified monks because of immigration rules. The problem? The monks had taken vows of poverty. The government didn't understand that the congregations were totally committed to supporting the monks and thought they'd be a burden to society at large. Temple building projects and activities have faced opposition from their neighbours in many Canadian cities. Mainstream media have panned the Dalai Lama and books about Canadian Buddhist history, and generally ignored Buddhist news altogether.

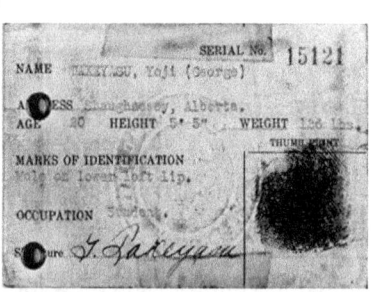

Journey of Spirit

"Journey of Spirit: A Buddhist monk bikes the Americas" is the Facebook Page[32] for Korean monk Daeung Sunim whose pilgrimage covered 20,000 miles circumnavigating North America and then down to the Southern tip of Argentina between 2012 and 2014. He set off East from Vancouver with no chase van, no contacts, no support network, no reservations, and no

---

32. https://www.facebook.com/JourneyOfSpirit

itinerary. He was met with open doors across Canada all the way to Nova Scotia.

2011

The Montreal Zen Poetry Festival held their 3rd annual event. Edo Japan Grill celebrated the opening of their 100th restaurant franchise location, in Edmonton. (So, what's the Buddhist connection? The chain was launched in Calgary in 1979 by Susumu Ikuta, a Buddhist minister who resigned in 1999 to become Bishop of the Buddhist Churches of Canada!) The 22nd Annual Montreal Tibetan Bazaar kicked into action in November. Dicki Chhoyang, a Tibetan Canadian from Montreal, became Minister for the Department of Information and International Relations in the 15th Tibetan Government in Exile in India.

Cults, Cons and Controversy

Buddhism in Canada has also seen its share of predatory community leaders, misguided devotees, political infighting, and stances that proved to be on the wrong side of history. It hasn't all been sweetness and light.

A hidden gem in Lethbridge, AB

During Canada's Centennial in 1967, Japanese Canadians came together to build the Nikka Yuko, a Japanese-style garden reflecting the magnificent mountain and prairie scenery of southern Alberta. It's still going strong and a vibrant attraction. There's also the amazing Nitobe Memorial Garden in Vancouver and the Japanese Botanical Garden in Montreal. We love Japanese gardens!

Photo courtesy of Ken Siever

Canada's Celebration of Japanese Architecture

Just north of Yonge and Bloor sits the Toronto Reference Library, designed by Moriyama+Teshima Architects. The library includes a vaulting interior vista and an open, inviting inner entrance featuring a babbling brook over riverstones to create the symbolic threshold between the world outside and the calm within. Moriyama was born in BC and was one of the Japanese Canadians interned during the war. He is known for his iconic landmarks, such as the Ontario Science Centre, the Bata Shoe Museum, the Canadian War Museum, Ottawa City Hall, many other projects.

Oh, there's more – lots more. The Sumeru Books blog has more than 1400 news stories like these about Buddhism in Canada.[33]

Are we there yet?

In another dimension from being a Buddhist book publisher, part of my day job includes being a high school Technological Design teacher, with a keen interest in teaching young people about project management (PM). I think PM skills are really important and not that hard to learn. There are many well-structured methodologies out there.

As I mentioned earlier, I've been thinking a lot about the future. To learn more, I've been reading extensively in the field of strategic foresight. That's what many organizations use to navigate, and it is also a very valuable skill to learn (given the volatility, uncertainty, complexity, and ambiguity of our future).

The interesting thing about strategic foresight isn't predicting what will happen (and being right or wrong). It's about creating holistic alternate scenarios of what *might* happen, what the drivers and tipping points will be, and the likely interactions of those complex systems. Within possible, probable, and preferred outcomes, we can be a bit more open to what may come and able to respond with calm, creativity, and presence.

Buddhist practice offers a unique vantagepoint from which to survey our prospects with a combination of wisdom, compassion, and belongingness in interbeing. It's not an escape from reality, not a nihilistic retreat into nothingness. Don't be fooled by the word "emptiness." I cannot think of a more robust philosophy to explain and navigate life than the Buddha's Eightfold Noble Path. (See Chapter 7)

I can't tell you what Canada's Buddhist organizations will look like in 2030 or 2050. That's up to you. Applying the tools of strategic foresight, I can imagine a variety of scenarios, and I offer you my sincere heartfelt bows of gratitude for your presence here, your energy. I am sure you will discover great truths and do great things in your lifetime. We are all gems creating together in Indra's Net.

---

33. https://sumeru-books.com/blogs/news

3 Life of the Buddha

Background

THE BUDDHA WAS A HUMAN BEING, not a god or a divine being. So he should not be compared with Yahweh in Judaism, God in Christianity, or Allah in Islam. Instead, it would be more appropriate to compare him to Jesus of Nazareth or the Prophet Muhammad, both of whom were born and lived on this earth, though in the Middle East, not on the Indian subcontinent.

The Buddha lived in the northeastern area of the Indian subcontinent some 2,600 years ago, about five hundred years before Jesus. Experts are divided on the exact years of his life: 624–544 BCE, 566–486, or 480–400. In this book, we will adopt the middle dates, that is to say, 566–486 BCE.

The records tell us that the Buddha was born a prince of a small kingdom of a clan called the "Shakya," located on the present-day borders of India and Nepal.[34] His given name was "Siddhartha," meaning "he whose purpose (*artha*) is accomplished (*siddha*)." His family name was "Gautama," which means the highest (*tama*) cow (*go*).

In Sanskrit, the main language from ancient India, the term "Buddha" means "one who has awakened" or the "Awakened One." So, "Buddha" is actually a title used to refer to anyone who attains ultimate spiritual Awakening, which is the goal of many Buddhists, past and present. So, this is true also for many Buddhists living in America and other parts of the world.

In other words, in Buddhism, there are as many "Buddhas" as there are awakened people. Yet, normally when we say "the Buddha," we are referring to the Indian prince who became the founder of Buddhism. To avoid any confusion, he is often referred to as "Shakyamuni Buddha"; "Shakya" in "Shakyamuni" refers to the name of his clan and "muni" means the "sage" (a person of wisdom). Thus, Shakyamuni means, "the sage of the Shakya Clan."

---

34. Kapilavathu, the place of the Buddha's birth, is considered to lie on the Nepalese side of the border as it is set today. Modern Nepalese insist that he was born in their country, but, of course, there was no border there at the time. So, it would be more accurate to say that Siddhartha Gautama was born on the "Indian subcontinent." It is in that sense that the term "India" or "Indian" will be used in this book.

Birth

Siddhartha Gautama was born to King Shuddhodana and Queen Maya. According to Buddhist legend, one night Queen Maya had a strange dream, in which she dreamed that a white elephant entered her womb through the right side of her chest.[35] Soon after, she learned that she had conceived a child. When it came time to give birth, Queen Maya set out to return to her parents' home to have the baby, in keeping with the custom of her day.

On her way, she took a rest in the Lumbini Garden, finding herself captivated by the beautiful flowers of the Ashoka trees. As she reached up for a branch of one of the trees, it is said that the tree bent down to meet her hand. She then gave birth in a standing position, while holding on to the branch for support.

As soon as her baby, the prince, was born, legend has it that he took seven steps. Then he pointed the right arm up and the left arm down and proclaimed, "In heavens above and heavens below, I alone am the honoured one!" In another version of the legend, he added: "This is my last birth. There will be no further rebirth."[36]

But the joy of his birth was short-lived, as Queen Maya suddenly died. The prince was, then, brought up by his aunt, his mother's younger sister, Mahaprajapati.

Childhood

By many accounts, the young prince was a sensitive child. Once, he sat under a tree, watching a farmer ploughing the field. Soon a bird swooped down to eat an earthworm. Then as the bird took to the sky, a huge bird attacked the smaller bird.

This shocked the sensitive young prince, and he was saddened by the fact that creatures have to hunt and eat others. Saddened, he whispered to himself, "Oh! Must all living creatures have to kill each other?" He felt deep

---

35. "Legends" are stories often written by later followers of extraordinary people and are not factual. They are often described as having super-human qualities, such as the Buddha's mother becoming pregnant through extra-ordinary ways, the Buddha walking as soon as being born, and making statements that seem to praise himself.

36. This means that he will become a Buddha in this life to become, as previously mentioned, free of the suffering of transmigration.

sadness for the plight of living creatures, even of earthworms and tiny birds.

Given the sensitive nature of the young prince, his father, King Shuddhodana, was probably not surprised when a hermit named Ashita prophesized that his son would be either a great king who would rule the four corners of the world or a great spiritual leader, the saviour of the world.

The father, of course, wanted his son to follow in his footsteps and to become a future king, but knowing the sensitive nature of Siddhartha, the king was fearful that his son might abandon the kingdom in favour of seeking the spiritual path. So, King Shuddhodana did everything in his power to shield the young prince from experiencing pain and suffering. The prince was surrounded only by young, healthy and beautiful people, and sheltered by a life of abundance and pleasure within the perfect setting inside the palace.

Excursions

However, this all came to an end when he wandered outside the palace gates four separate times, which came to be known as the "Excursions from the Four Gates," or "the Four Messengers."

On his first journey, accompanied by his driver, Prince Siddhartha rode out from the east gate of the palace in a chariot. He then came upon a very old person, bent over and barely able to walk even with a cane. The prince had never seen anyone like him before since he knew only young people. So, the prince was puzzled and asked the driver who the strange looking person could be. The driver explained that he was an elderly man and that everyone would be like him if one lived long enough. Shocked, the prince asked, "I, too?" and the reply was, "Yes, you too, sir."

On another day, the prince left the palace from the south gate. Shortly thereafter, the prince came upon a very sick person lying on the side of the road in great pain and agony. The prince had never seen anyone like him before since he had surrounded himself with only healthy people.

So, the prince was puzzled and asked the driver what was happening to the person who was in pain. The driver then explained that he was sick and that virtually everyone would get sick if one lived long enough. Shocked, the prince asked, "I, too?" and the reply was, "Yes, you too, sir."

The prince left the palace yet a third time from the west gate. He came upon a dead person surrounded by his family and friends who were wailing and crying, overcome with grief. The prince had never seen people in grief as well as the body of a deceased person, since he had lived only with young and healthy people.

So, the prince was puzzled and asked the driver why the body lay so still and why the people were crying. The driver explained that the person had died and that everyone eventually dies. Shocked once more, he asked, "I, too?" and the reply was, "Yes, you too, sir."

On another day, the prince left from the north gate, where he came upon a different scene from the past three excursions. He came upon a wandering monk. The monk's serenity and inner glow captivated the prince. So the prince asked the driver who this person was, and how the monk had become so peaceful looking.

The driver then explained that he was a monk who had abandoned ordinary life to seek a spiritual life. The prince was strangely attracted to the monk to such an extent that he wanted to be like him. As a young man, he felt he had found what he wanted to do in life.

For Prince Siddhartha, the four excursions outside the castle walls were a series of life-changing experiences that influenced the decision he later took, leading to the next phase of his life.

Leaving Home

After the excursion experience, the prince was tormented as he debated within himself about his future course. After some time went by, at the age of 29, the prince decided to pursue the life of a monk in hope of finding a way to overcome human suffering. Leaving home was, however, a very difficult decision, for not only would he be abandoning his role as the future king and disappointing his father, but by now the prince was married and had a newborn son named Rahula.

The prince had taken a wife named Yashodara, a princess from a neighbouring country. It was an arranged marriage in keeping with the custom of that time. They were happily married and were now blessed with a baby boy, making the prince's decision to leave them even more tormenting.

In a heartbreaking scene, Siddhartha wanted to hold his son for the last time but stopped himself, for he did not want to awaken his wife, as this would have made his departure immensely more difficult. As he left the room, the prince looked one last time toward his wife and son, fighting back his emotions.

Today we may look at his actions as being uncaring and selfish, but it was customary in those days for spiritual seekers to leave their homes. However, most of them did so much later in life, unlike Siddhartha, who was in the prime of his life at the age of 29. But Siddhartha was extraordinary, for he wanted desperately to find a way out of suffering, not only for himself but also for all humanity, especially for his loved ones.

As Siddhartha got ready to leave the castle, his servant Channa prepared a white horse, Kanthaka, for the departure. The prince had Channa accompany him till he arrived at the border of the kingdom, where he cut off his lock of hair and took off his royal apparel in exchange for a simple garment of a spiritual seeker. He then asked Channa to return to the castle with the horse. Having to part with his master, Channa was deeply saddened and wept openly. Siddhartha comforted Channa repeatedly, asking him to inform the family left behind that he was all right and that they should not worry.

Ascetic Practice

After seeing Channa off, Siddhartha began his search. From this point on, he was no longer a prince but rather an ascetic dedicated to finding spiritual Awakening. He could also be called "Bodhisattva," meaning the "seeker of Awakening."[37] His search led him to two kinds of rigourous discipline, first meditation and then later, austerities.

---

37. "Bodhisattva" does also refer to those who have attained high states of Awakening especially in Mahayana Buddhism, but this is a usage used in early Buddhism particularly when referring to Prince Siddhartha as a spiritual seeker.

He first studied with a teacher named Arada Kalama, who taught him a form of meditation called "attainment of the state of nothing at all." Siddhartha practiced diligently and quickly mastered it, but it did not lead him to the goal that he was seeking.

Then, he went to learn another form of meditation called the "attainment of neither perception nor non-perception" taught by another famous teacher, Udraka Ramaputra. Again, Siddhartha quickly mastered it and even became one of the teachers of this method, but again he was not satisfied.

Having found both meditation methods that led to deep internal states of calm and concentration ultimately unsatisfying, Siddhartha decided to try physical austerities or extreme hardship. He learned to survive on one grain of rice and one drop of water a day. These ascetic practices aimed at weakening the strength of the body in order to allow the inner pure spirit to be freed from the bonds of the flesh. It is said that this decision was, in part, a reaction to the life of luxury and physical pleasure of the palace that he had left behind.

The austere practices were so demanding that his body became extremely emaciated or thin, to the point where his arms and legs became so thin that, in his words, they were like "the jointed stems of creepers or bamboo," and his eyes sank deep in their sockets like "the gleam of water seen deep down at the bottom of a deep well."

Unfortunately, yet again, he was making no progress whatsoever, giving him no choice but to abandon these austere practices. Hence, both his life of pleasure in the palace and the six years of ascetic life in the forest could not bring peace.

Awakening (Enlightenment or Nirvana)

Siddhartha came to the realization that he needed to avoid the extremes. He had taken up the austerities as a reaction to the life of luxury and satisfaction of desires he had known in the palace, but had gone too far in depriving himself of food and sleep. A healthy body was, of course, important. So, he decided to receive an offering of milk and rice offered by a young woman named Sujata from a nearby village.

Having regained his physical strength, Siddhartha, the Bodhisattva, sat under a Pipal tree, which came to be called "the tree of Awakening" or

Bodhi tree, and resolved not to leave the spot until he had realized the state of Awakening. In the shade of the tree, he then settled into a state of deep meditative calm and peace.

There are many accounts of what actually took place, but one that many find easy to understand and appreciate is explained in a story of the Bodhisattva's encounter with a figure called Mara. Mara means "the bringer of death," and one that symbolizes our mental and emotional attachment. In this tale, Mara appeared before the Bodhisattva with various temptations to get the Bodhisattva to give in to his greed, hatred and ignorance.

For example, Mara sent an army of demons to attack him with many kinds of weapons. However, Siddhartha perceived the demons and their weapons as representing the attachment of hatred and anger. Consequently, he did not react to them and so the rain of weapons hurled at him by the demons turned into a rain of beautiful flowers. In this way, the Bodhisattva saw that people suffer because they let these attachments run wild and overwhelm them.

Mara then approached Siddhartha directly to challenge him and asked, by what right did he sit under the tree of Awakening? Siddhartha replied, by the right of having practiced the spiritual path for a long time. Mara countered him by saying that he, too, had done the same. Besides which, he had all his armies to vouch or be his witness for this fact; but who, he asked, could vouch for Siddhartha?

Siddhartha, the Bodhisattva, then, touched the ground with his right hand, calling on the very Earth as witness in what has come to be known as the "earth-touching gesture." This signaled Mara's defeat and Siddhartha, the

Bodhisattva's Awakening as the Buddha.[38]

This is obviously not the whole story of the Buddha's Awakening, but rather gives us a glimpse into the nature of that Awakening, as described in the scriptures:

> When the morning star appeared in the eastern sky, the struggle was over and the Bodhisattva's mind was as clear and bright as the breaking day. He had, at last, found the path to Awakening. He had become the "Awakened One," the Buddha!

This Awakening is also referred to as "enlightenment" or "nirvana." Nirvana means "the state where one's flame of greed, hatred and ignorance has been blown out." For your information, Nirvana is now considered an English word and even became the name of two internationally famous rock bands, one British and the other American.[39]

In this Awakening, the Buddha had directly experienced Truth, which the Indians called "Dharma." He found himself in a sublime and peaceful state beyond anything that any words could describe. But most importantly, the Buddha had gained full understanding about the nature of suffering, the cause of suffering, and the way to overcome suffering. This, if you recall, was the very reason why he pursued the spiritual path, even as he sacrificed his family and the throne.

Teachings

We are told that the Buddha spent some weeks enjoying the bliss of Awakening under and near the Bodhi tree or the tree of Awakening. He also felt hesitant to share the insights of his Awakening with others because he saw that the people in the world would not be able to understand them. The people were, in the Buddha's view, too attached or caught up with the matters of the world to comprehend what he would have to say about the Dharma.

Then, Brahma, the Hindu god, appeared before the Buddha to request him to teach the Dharma for the sake of those who would be interested. Encouraged by Brahma that there would be some people who might be able to comprehend his words, the Buddha decided to share his insights.

Once he decided to share what he had discovered, the Buddha walked some 100 miles to the city of Benares. In the Deer Park in the nearby town of Saranath, he met up with the five fellow monks with whom he had trained together during the period of austere practices.

---

38. This implies that the Buddha's witness (Earth itself) was superior to Mara's witness (his armies).

39. The British band was formed in 1965 and the American band in 1987.

At first, they shunned him for they saw him as a "quitter," who had quit the austere practices. However, soon Buddha's demeanour and his words won them over as they heard the Buddha deliver his first sermon, centred on his core teaching, the Four Noble Truths.[40] (See Chapter 6)

Empowered by the authentic virtues of his Awakening and guided by the skilfulness of his teaching, they listened earnestly and soon attained Awakening. They, then, became the Buddha's first disciples and began to form the Sangha, the order of monks and nuns.

From that point on, the Buddha journeyed around several kingdoms of Northeast India to share his teachings. His personal qualities of charisma and compassion led many to seek him as their teacher. Many became his disciples, and the size of the Sangha swelled. According to some accounts, even his wife, Yashodhara, his son, Rahula, his stepmother, Mahaprajapati, and his father, Shuddhodana also joined the Sangha.

Despite his initial hesitation to share, the Buddha dedicated the rest of his life to traveling throughout the region in order to teach. Over the course of 45 years of teaching, the Buddha inspired numerous ordinary people as well as monks and nuns who formed the Sangha.

Passing

When he was 80 years old, he became ill after accepting a meal which contained either pork or mushrooms, offered by a smith named Chunda. Illness caused intense pain and bleeding, but the Buddha kept walking toward

---

40. This sermon is found the *Sutra of the Setting in Motion the Wheel of Dharma*.

his next destination. Arriving in the town of Kushinagara, he lay down between two large Sala trees. Despite his illness, he continued to teach until the last moments of life.

When asked by his disciples what should be done after he passed away, the Buddha replied that rather than saying prayers and making offerings to his body, he encouraged them to focus on their own practice. Seeing his disciples, lay supporters and even the animals weeping amid the sadness of the imminent death of their teacher, the Buddha spoke these famous words to comfort and encourage them to strive harder:

> Make yourself the light. Rely upon yourself. Do not depend upon anyone else. Make my teachings your light.

The Buddha did not choose a successor in a particular individual but told his disciples to regard his teachings, the Dharma, which he had shared for the past 45 years, to serve as the guide after his death.

Sensing that his end was approaching he entered a state of deep meditation and took his last breath calmly and peacefully. The Buddha had entered *complete* nirvana (*pari-nirvana*), in which the passions of the physical body had also become completely extinguished. He had attained the ultimate state beyond all suffering. At that point, the legends tell us that the Earth shook and a thundering sound was heard from the heavens.

4 A Brief History of Buddhism in Asia

TODAY THERE ARE TWO major branches of Buddhism. One is called the Theravada (School of Elders), which is dominant in Sri Lanka, Myanmar (Burma), Thailand, Cambodia, and Laos. The other is called the Mahayana (the Larger Vehicle), which is practiced in China, Japan, Korea, Mongolia, Taiwan, Tibet, and Vietnam. Both branches trace their roots to the original teachings of Shakyamuni Buddha. The Buddha himself belonged to no specific school, just as Jesus was not Roman Catholic, Eastern Orthodox or Protestant.

Early Years

Soon after the death of the Buddha in around 486 BCE, his disciples of the Sangha (the community of monks and nuns) gathered in a large council to determine and preserve his teachings. Ananda, a disciple who was at the Buddha's side for the last twenty years of life, took the lead in reciting the teachings that he had heard from the Buddha.

These teachings were then memorized, preserved and transmitted to future generations, without being put into writing. These teachings would be transmitted orally for about four hundred years! They were finally put *into writing* around the beginning of the Common Era or about the time Jesus of Nazareth was born.

During the one hundred years after the passing of the Buddha, the disciples spread the teachings to a wider area of the Northeastern part of the Indian subcontinent. Consequently, when the second council was gathered around 386 BCE, the Sangha had been divided into 18 schools. Each of the schools had developed its own emphasis on the parts of the teachings and practices that were important to it.

Around 268 BCE, King Ashoka took reign over much of the Indian subcontinent. He strongly supported the Buddhist religion by carving the teachings on high stone pillars that he erected throughout his empire. These pillars have been unearthed in modern times and have served as a valuable resource for Buddhist history. The King uplifted the living conditions of his people by building medical clinics and making traveling easier by building hostels and planting trees along travel roads.

King Ashoka helped to spread the Buddhist teachings beyond India by sending missionaries to the neighbouring countries. He even sent his own son, Mahinda, to Sri Lanka, which marks the beginning of Buddhism in that country. We shall discuss a bit later the spread of Buddhism to Sri Lanka and to other countries, but we still need to say a few words about how Buddhism continued to develop on the Indian subcontinent.

Mahayana Branch in India

Around the beginning of the Common Era, around 450 years after the death of the Buddha, a new form of Buddhism called the Mahayana (larger vehicle) began to emerge. This movement was separate from the 18 earlier schools, as its leaders believed that their teachings expressed the true *intent* of what the Buddha taught. In their view, all beings have the potential to become Buddhas, and they called this potentiality "Buddha nature." This Buddha nature is none other than the "gem within" emphasized in this book.

The Mahayana sought to embrace *all* people by including the laypersons more on an equal footing with the monks and nuns. So, they thought of themselves as the "Greater Vehicle" and criticized some of the eighteen earlier schools by calling them the "Hinayana" (Smaller Vehicle).

Consequently, some people, even today, refer to Theravada Buddhism in Sri Lanka and Southeast Asia as the "Smaller Vehicle." This should be avoided for two reasons. It is historically wrong to call it by that name.[41] And secondly, it is ethically wrong to use a negative name to refer to other groups, especially when the Theravada Buddhists are just as concerned about the welfare of all beings as are the Mahayana Buddhists.

Admittedly, Mahayana Buddhists have emphasized more than the Theravada Buddhists the idea that laypersons can realize Awakening, not just monks and nuns. For example, an Awakened layperson by the name of Vimalakirti is well-known for having taught even famous monks about the deeper truth in the Buddhist teachings.

Vimalakirti was considered to be a Bodhisattva.[42] The Bodhisattvas were a category of Awakened people whom the Mahayana Buddhists aspired to become. The actions of the Bodhisattvas were motivated by their

---

41. The Theravada Buddhists had left India for Sri Lanka at least a couple of a hundred years before the Mahayana Buddhists came on the scene.

42. Here the term "Bodhisattva" means those who attained higher levels of Awakening and is not being used in exactly the same sense as when referring to Siddhartha before becoming the Buddha.

compassion for other beings, so much so that they voluntarily put off becoming Buddhas themselves in order to stay in the world to assist all beings to attain Awakening.[43]

A number of Mahayana branches developed within the next five hundred years in India, mostly centred on specific sutras (Buddhist texts) or sets of sutras. For example, the *Perfection of Wisdom Sutras* led to the formation of the Middle Way school, which was founded by Nagarjuna (around 150–250). Another set of sutras that included the *Sandhinirmocana Sutra* inspired a school called the Consciousness-Only School. Two brothers, Asanga and Vasubandhu (around 400), were the key figures of this school.

The *Garland Sutra*, *Lotus Sutra*, *Nirvana Sutra* and the *Larger Pure Land Sutra*, on the other hand, did not contribute to the formation of a doctrinally based school in India. However, their teachings of universal salvation, the depictions of the realms of Awakening, and their aesthetically inspiring images have generated a large following and continue to this day to have major influence where Mahayana Buddhism has spread.

Despite the flourishing of Mahayana forms, we must not forget that some of the earlier schools of Buddhism continue to exist throughout India. The monks and nuns of these schools continued to keep their monasteries thriving and contributed to the establishment of centres of learning such as Nalanda and Vikramashila. Nalanda was built as early as the sixth century and can be seen as one of the earliest "universities" in the world.

From around the sixth century a distinct form of teaching called Tantra or Vajrayana (diamond vehicle) became popular throughout India and most of the Buddhist world. It has been particularly strong in Tibet and continues to be so today. Some scholars regard this as the third branch of Buddhism, separate from Theravada and Mahayana, while others see it as part of the Mahayana. We agree with the second group of scholars, so shall mention it briefly here as part of the Mahayana branch.

Buddhist Tantra is a form of mysticism mixed with magic. Magic includes spells or sacred words, which when recited were believed to protect people from such dangers as snakebites. Buddhists also incorporated from Hinduism sacred sounds such as "Aum" (pronounced "Ooum"). Besides these sacred words, Buddhist Tantra adopted magic circles or *mandalas*, which were used in rituals in which the meditator sought to become the deity (gods, supernatural beings) that he or she conjured up.

All of these features are difficult to fully understand without experiencing them ourselves, but two other distinct features of Buddhist Tantra were

---

43. In this context, it was thought that once a person became a Buddha, he or she would teach for some time but eventually go beyond this world. But some elected to remain in this world, who were then referred to as "Bodhisattvas."

1) the necessity of having a personal teacher, a guru, and 2) the view that the world is *essentially* pure. With such features, to practice Tantra was not for ordinary Buddhist followers but for the highly trained. Nevertheless, Tantric Buddhism played a dominant role starting around 600 CE.

Starting in the sixth century, Buddhism began its gradual decline in India, particularly in the northern areas such as Gandhara and Kashmir. Buddhism lasted longer in the Ganges valley, but it gradually fell victim to the forces that weakened its existence. One such force was the expansion of Muslim influence that proved detrimental to Buddhism. In 1198, Nalanda University was burned down and ceased to exist a few decades later. Vikramashila, the other major centre of learning, ceased to exist soon after.

These losses were not the only reason for the eventual disappearance of Buddhism from the land of its birth. Buddhists themselves are to be blamed. Because the kings and ruling groups were Buddhism's main supporters, the Buddhist institutions became less concerned with the needs of ordinary people. So, when they lost royal support or were destroyed by outside forces, there was no strong popular support to rebuild and support Buddhist institutions.

And Buddhism gradually came to be *absorbed* by Hinduism, the dominant religion on the Indian subcontinent. For example, Buddha has become one of the manifestations (avatars) of the Hindu God, Vishnu.

Let us now look at how Buddhism spread beyond India. For that, we must go back to the time of King Ashoka in the third century BCE. As you recall, King Asoka unified the Indian subcontinent and became a strong supporter of Buddhism and helped to spread it beyond India.

Buddhism in Sri Lanka and Southeast Asia

Sri Lanka

The Buddhism that Mahinda, King Ashoka's son, transmitted was the Theravada or the School of Elders, one of the eighteen schools. King Tissa of Sri Lanka adopted Buddhism and helped in its spread throughout the island. Soon Buddhism became the state religion.

In the early 11th century, the Tamils from India conquered the island. This severely disrupted the Sangha, the order of Buddhist monks and nuns. A huge casualty of the conquest was the women's order of nuns, whose line of transmission was severed. This prevented new nuns from being ordained in the country.[44]

Within several decades, the Tamils were driven out with the aid of the

---

44. Ordination requires a proper ritual with a minimum number of nuns, but the disruptions from the foreign occupation prevented it.

Burmese (people of Myanmar), who also helped to revive the men's order of monks. The Burmese were able to provide the monks required for carrying out the ordination. On the other hand, the women's order was unfortunately unable to revive itself. However, in recent years, after close to one thousand years, the order of nuns in Sri Lanka has been revived with the assistance of the order of nuns from Taiwan.

From the 16th century, Buddhism again was weakened as the Portuguese, the Dutch and finally the British colonized Sri Lanka. But from the late 1800s a movement began to revitalize Buddhism by debating the Christians and strengthening the Buddhist disciplines and teachings.

This movement was helped by the support of an American Buddhist, Henry Steel Olcott, who was mentioned earlier and will be discussed later in relation to American Buddhism. Olcott is highly respected even today for his contribution to the revival of Buddhism in Sri Lanka, which continues to be the dominant religion in Sri Lanka.

Myanmar (Burma)

Buddhism was first introduced to Burma when King Ashoka sent monks as missionaries in the middle of the third century BCE. From that point on, Buddhist presence grew and began to play an important role in the country. Buddhism gained prominence during the period of the Pagan kingdom (849–1287), when the kings supported Theravada Buddhism while turning away the influx of Hinduism, Mahayana Buddhism and Tantric Buddhism.

During the reign of King Anawrahta (1040–1077), Burma became the most thriving centre of Buddhism in South and Southeast Asia. For example, it was during this time that monks were sent to Sri Lanka to help restore their ordination line, which was threatened by extinction. The capital of Pagan was transformed by the building of numerous magnificent religious structures, eventually boasting close to 10,000 pagodas (*stupas*) and temples. Its splendour was known in Europe through the writings of Marco Polo.

From that point on, for close to a millennium, Theravada Buddhism has remained strong through centuries of monarchy, British colonization and the post-World War II period. Today, the monasteries and temples play a prominent role in the religious lives of the people of Myanmar. Myanmar's form of Buddhism is especially known for its strength in meditation, thus, drawing many from the West and other Asian countries seeking training in authentic meditative practices.

Cambodia, Thailand and Laos

Because of their intimate historical connections, we will consider the three countries together. First, with regard to Cambodia, Buddhism first arrived there as early the first century CE, and by the fifth century, Buddhism of the Mahayana branch existed side by side with Hinduism. The rulers for the next seven hundred years supported both religions, which are reflected at the world-famous site, the Angkor Wat with its motifs of both religions.

In the late 12th century, a Burmese monk introduced the Theravada branch of Buddhism to Cambodia. Within one hundred years, Theravada Buddhism had supplanted the Mahayana variety to become the dominant form of Buddhism in Cambodia. The Khmer kings also dropped their support of Hinduism in favour of Theravada Buddhism, which then went on to become the dominant religion of the Cambodian people up to the present.

As for Thailand, Theravada Buddhism was introduced from Burma to Thailand in the 13th century, with the emergence of a strong kingdom headed by King Ramkham-haeng. A couple of centuries later in the 15th century, the kings adopted Hindu ceremonies and law, but Buddhism continued to be strong among the ordinary people.

Buddhism continued to thrive in Thailand, so much so that in the 18th century monks from Sri Lanka turned to Thailand as a source of knowledge and the ordination transmission line for revitalizing Sri Lankan Buddhism. To this day, Buddhism continues to be the Thai national religion, symbolized by the custom of requiring the king of Thailand to be ordained for a brief period as a Buddhist monk.

As in Burma and Cambodia, Laotian people's earliest encounter with Buddhism was with Mahayana Buddhism. But in the 14th century, Theravada Buddhism was introduced from Cambodia at the time of the founding of the first Laotian state. Supported by subsequent kings, Theravada became the official religion of Laos. Today, over 95 percent of the people in Laos are Buddhist.

Malaysia and Indonesia

Theravada Buddhism is also found in Malaysia and Indonesia, where its presence is very small compared to the other Southeast Asian countries already discussed. These two countries are interesting in that the Buddhists find themselves in societies where Islam is the dominant religion.

Buddhism along with Hinduism entered Indonesia as early as the second century. Today, Buddhism is considered one of Indonesia's six officially recognized religions. Its followers make up about one percent of the population, and the vast majority of the Buddhists are ethnic Chinese. The memories of Buddhism in the ancient history of this country are symbolized by the magnificent, world-famous stupa at Borobudur on the island of Java.

Buddhism entered Malaysia also in the second century CE, brought over by priests as well as by merchants. Today, Buddhists are much more numerous in Malaysia than in Indonesia, as Buddhism is the second largest religion. Buddhists make up about 20 percent of the entire population and most of them are involved in business and various professions, living in the urban areas. As in Indonesia, most of the Buddhists are of Chinese heritage, and they also practice other forms of Chinese religions including Confucianism and Daoism.

The role of monks

We have presented an overview of Buddhism in Southeast Asia, where the Theravada branch is dominant. When asked what the main characteristic of Theravada Buddhism is, I would point to the important role of the monks. Perhaps you have seen the scenes of saffron-robed monks meditating in the monasteries or on their morning rounds of collecting alms in the streets with their "begging bowls."

These monks are considered to be in the best position to realize Awakening in this life. The laypersons play the role of supporters, in the hope that in future lives they will become monks or nuns themselves. They believe that when they donate meals and robes to the monks and money to the temples, they are creating "merit" which will help them have lives of inner peace and good fortune.

On a personal note, many years ago when I was 23 years old, I, too, led the life of a novice monk for a couple of months in a monastery in Bangkok, Thailand. (See its photo at the back of this book.) I still have many fond memories, particularly of the stillness of the predawn hours, the aroma of the food being placed in my alms bowl, the genuine devotion of the lay supporters, and the coolness of the ground as my bare feet paced mindfully through the town streets.

I have nothing but respect for the monks who dedicate their lives to overcome greed, hatred, and ignorance. I admire their self-reliance, for they exemplify the Buddha's final words:

> Make yourself the light. Rely upon yourself. Do not depend upon anyone else.

We have now looked at how Buddhism spread to Sri Lanka and Southeast Asian countries. Now we shall explore how Buddhism spread north to China and to other East Asian countries mostly by land via the caravan routes, which later came to be known as the "Silk Route."

Buddhism in China, Taiwan, Vietnam, Korea, and Japan

China

Buddhism entered China in the first century CE, mostly through the silk routes of Central Asia.[45] Buddhism remained a "foreign" minor religion for a few centuries. Then in the fifth century, the Northern Wei Dynasty adopted Buddhism as its state religion.

From the fifth century Buddhism received the support of various dynasties. Then in the seventh century, Buddhism, along with Confucianism and Daoism, became the state religion of the Tang Dynasty (618–907). During this period in China, Buddhism experienced its golden age.

During this dynasty, the number of Buddhist temples and monks and nuns grew enormously. Buddhism received not only the support of the emperors but also that of the ordinary people. This supportive environment led to the emergence of many different Buddhist schools, such as Tientai, Huayan, Faxiang and Chenyan.

But the two schools that have been the most popular are the Pure Land and Chan (or "Zen" in its Japanese pronunciation) schools. While the other schools mentioned above developed sophisticated doctrine, these two schools have been the most popular because they represent the two main forms of practice. The two forms of *practice* are meditation (Chan), mostly for monks and nuns, and recitation (Pure Land) of the name of Buddha Omituofo (Amitabha) mostly for the lay followers.

Since the Tang period, for over a thousand years, Buddhism has endured many ups and downs but has remained one of the main religions of China. It has survived the numerous persecutions, including the latest one in the 1960s during the Cultural Revolution. However, conditions have improved since the 1970s, due to economic prosperity and the government's easing of restrictions on religion. Buddhism has benefitted enormously within this environment. For example, the numbers of monks and nuns have increased and so has the financial support of the temples.

---

45. Recent studies are showing that there was much more transmission of Buddhism to China from the southern sea route than previously thought. A good example is Bodhidharma, who brought Zen (Chan) Buddhism to China.

Taiwan

Buddhism has enjoyed a better environment there than in mainland China, and it has become the dominant religion of this island country. Centred on a few dominant temples, such as Buddha Light Mountain (Foguang Shan), Dharma Drum Mountain (Fagu Shan), Compassion Society (Tzu Chi), and Chung Tai Monastery, Buddhism has met the needs of a prosperous contemporary society.

These institutions have built colleges and hospitals and made concerted effort in social welfare and disaster relief work. They promote what some call "humanistic Buddhism" in their effort to emphasize the *present* life over life *after* death. This has inspired the spirit of socially-engaged Buddhism and efforts to build a "Pure Land on Earth."

Vietnam

Buddhism entered Vietnam as early as the second century CE, via routes that stretched from India to Central Asia. As ties to China strengthened, the Chinese forms of Buddhism influenced Buddhism in Vietnam, which coexisted with and, at times, incorporated preexisting indigenous beliefs and practices.

After gaining independence from China in 968, the subsequent ruling dynasties of Le, Ly and Tran (980–1400) fully supported Buddhism. During this period, the Zen (Thien) school became the dominant form of Buddhism especially in the courts and the monasteries. Among the populace, Pure Land Buddhism centred on Buddha A-di-da (Amitabha) became widely practiced. It requires mentioning that the Theravada form of Buddhism also continues to exist in Vietnam, mostly in the south.

One of the hallmarks of Vietnamese Buddhism, particularly in the modern period, is the emphasis on participating in the affairs of the world. The French colonialists and the communists did not favour and even persecuted the Buddhists. Many of us still remember with horror the Buddhist monks who engaged in self-immolation (burning), dying in the streets of Saigon (the capital at the time). They made the ultimate sacrifice as demonstration of their protest against the persecution directed at the Buddhists.

And during the decades of armed conflict, including the Vietnam War in which the United States was involved for nearly ten years, some Buddhist monks became actively involved in alleviating the suffering of the people. One such noted monk was Thich Nhat Hanh, who decided that monks needed to be involved in the world and who is credited with coining the now often-utilized term, "socially-engaged Buddhism."

Korea

Buddhism was introduced to the Korean peninsula in the fourth century from China. At the time, Korea was divided into three kingdoms, Kogurio to the north, Paekche in the southwest, and Silla in the southeast. All three actively adopted Buddhism as a way to unify their kingdom and to adopt culture and technology from China.

When the entire Korean peninsula was unified under the Silla dynasty, Buddhism received even greater support. This supportive environment led to the emergence of eminent scholar-monks who wrote first-rate commentaries on the sutras and also led to the spread of Buddhism among the populace.

One such eminent monk was Wonhyo, whose writings are considered superb and whose work influenced Buddhist thinkers in China. Wonhyo is rather unique in that he left the monkhood to get married and even had a child. He further popularized Buddhism by spreading the practice of chanting the name of Amitabha.

Buddhism lost its political support in Korea with the Joseon dynasty (1392–1897), which opted to support Confucianism. Buddhists were severely persecuted, Buddhist temples destroyed, and monks ousted. The impact of this persecution was severe, due to the fact that the Joseon dynasty lasted for about five hundred years. However, Buddhism managed to survive and has emerged in the modern period to be one of Korea's dominant religions.

Today Buddhists make up about 40 percent of the population, compared to an equal number of Christians. It is said that the Buddhists are older and live in the rural areas, compared to the Christians, who tend to be younger and live in the urban areas.

The Chogye school is the largest school of Korean Buddhism. They sponsor modern universities, such as Dongguk University, which boasts a medical school with hospitals inspired by Buddhist teachings and practice. There has been the emergence of a number of new Buddhist groups such as Won Buddhism, which seek to meet the needs of contemporary society. One such need has been the interest in meditation.

Japan

Buddhism first arrived in Japan in the middle of the sixth century, when King Seong of the Korean kingdom of Paekche sent some Buddhist scrolls and a small statue of a Buddha to Emperor Kinmei of Japan. This set off a struggle in Japan between the two factions of leadership, one that supported the adoption of Buddhism and the other that opposed it.

By the beginning of the seventh century the pro-Buddhist group, led by Prince Shotoku, won out. The prince drafted the Seventeen Article Constitution that aimed to unite the burgeoning nation by adopting Buddhist principles, including the "Three Treasures" of Buddha, Dharma and Sangha.

The government continued to play a vital role in utilizing Buddhism as a way of uniting the nation by establishing a central temple in Nara that had administrative oversight over the regional temples throughout Japan. Monks were called upon to serve as advisers as well as to pray for the peace and prosperity of the nation.

In the ninth century, eminent monks Saicho and Kukai studied in China and returned to establish the Tendai and Shingon schools, respectively. These schools then spawned new traditions in the 12th and 13th centuries, such as the Pure Land, Zen and Nichiren schools, whose members today make up the majority of the Buddhists in Japan.

During the past 1,000 years, Buddhism has coexisted with Shinto, Japan's indigenous religion. This has resulted in most Japanese households having both a Buddhist altar and a Shinto shrine in their homes. Buddhism has also served to produce artistic and cultural traditions including tea and flower arranging ceremonies.

Buddhism in Tibet and Mongolia

Tibet

Even though Tibet is close to India, Buddhism entered Tibet relatively late in the seventh century during the reign of King Srong Tseng Ganpo. Buddhism helped the king to consolidate his power and to establish a strong spiritual foundation for his reign.

In Tibet, Buddhism managed to strike a cooperative relationship with the indigenous religion, Bon. This relationship has characterized some of the unique qualities of Tibetan Buddhism, which is sometimes referred to as "Bon Buddhism" and its monks as "lamas."

By the mid-eighth century, Buddhism from China had begun to make its presence felt. On the other hand, the presence of Indian Buddhism was strengthened by the arrival of the eminent monk Padmasambhava from India. This led the Tibetans to make a decision as to which form of Buddhism to adopt. They did this by holding a series of debates at Samye Monastery.

At this historical set of debates, Indian Buddhism was represented by Kamalashila and Chinese Buddhism by a Chan master, Hvashan Mahayana. The former represented a more "gradual" approach while the latter represented a more "sudden" approach to enlightenment. Both put up a great fight, and in the end the Tibetans chose Buddhism from India.

From this point on in Tibet, Indian Buddhism continued to evolve through four major schools, the Nyingma, Kagyu, Sakya and Gelug. Of the four, Gelugpa is best known for its leader, whose title is the Dalai Lama. The first Dalai Lama lived in the 17th century. According to this tradition, it is thought that the previous Dalai Lama is reborn as the next Dalai Lama. Accordingly, Tenzin Gyatso, the current Dalai Lama, who is the 14th Dalai Lama, is considered to be the reincarnation of the 13th Dalai Lama.

In 1959, the current Dalai Lama had to leave Tibet due to the occupation by the Chinese military, which claimed Tibet as part of their territory. He has lived in exile in India ever since but has traveled the world to promote Buddhism and peace.

He continues to be highly respected by others, as witnessed by his being awarded the Nobel Peace Prize in 1989 for his environmental work, Honorary Canadian Citizenship in 2006, and the United States Congressional Gold Medal in 2007. (See his photo on p 174.) His numerous travels to the West are filled with speaking engagements, which are attended by thousands of people of all religions.

Mongolia

Buddhism entered Mongolia in a piecemeal fashion starting in the early centuries of the first millennium CE, from the various adjacent regions, such as Nepal and Central Asia. Then, it was in the Yuan dynasty (1271–1368) when the Mongols ruled China that the emperors converted to the Tibetan form of Buddhism. Buddhism became the state religion of the Mongol empire.

After the end of the Yuan dynasty, the Mongols reverted to their indigenous shamanistic form of religion. Later, in the 16th century, Mongolia once again turned to Buddhism as its religious foundation through the efforts of rulers such as Altan Khan. It was he who recognized the leader of the Gelug school of Tibetan Buddhism and bestowed upon him the title "Dalai Lama"; this title has survived to the present, with the 14th Dalai Lama as mentioned earlier. As these close ties with Tibetan Buddhism show, Buddhism played a dominant role among the Mongols through the Yuan period.

During the Qing dynasty (1635–1912) in China, the ruling people, the Manchus, supported the Tibetan form of Buddhism. However, the Qing rulers used Buddhism mostly as a means of controlling the Mongolians and Tibetans. Nevertheless, Buddhism has continued to play an important role in the spiritual lives of many ordinary Mongolians into the modern period. Since the overthrow of the Communists in 1990, there has been a resurgence of Buddhism. In 2010, 53 percent of Mongolians identified themselves as Buddhists.[46]

From Asia to North America

As we have seen in this chapter, Buddhism spread eastward through much of Asia over the past 2,600 years. However, during the same time Buddhism did not travel westward from the Indian subcontinent to take root in Europe or North America as a living religion for a large number of people.

Finally, starting in the 19th century, Buddhism climbed over the "Western wall" to establish itself as a living religion among diverse groups of people. And the Buddhism that arrived in North America came from *all* of the Asian countries that were described above.

---

46. 2010 Population and Housing Census of Mongolia. Data recorded in Brian J. Grim et al., *Yearbook of International Religious Demography 2014*. BRILL, 2014. p. 152.

5 A Brief History of Buddhism in Canada

Durgesh Kasbekar

THE HISTORY of Buddhism in Canada is younger than that of the United States. In the U.S., Buddhism's history began in 1844 on the East Coast among the intellectuals. Buddhism found its way to the USA from Europe, where scholars had been studying and learning about it for a century. We can, perhaps, call this "intellectual" Buddhism, which was confined to academics and intellectuals. Canada did not have such a tradition of "intellectual Buddhism" as compared to the U.S.

This can be attributed to three reasons. First, Canada is younger than the U.S. by around ninety years. It came into being in 1867 as an entity independent of British governance. Nation building was a drawn-out process as other provinces continued to join Canada as late as 1949.[47] On the other hand, by 1867, the year Canada was formed, the U.S. saw Nebraska join as its 37th state.[48] Second, unlike the U.S., Canada did not have institutions such as the American Oriental Society and conferences such as the 1893 World Parliament of Religions held in Chicago, which was attended by numerous Buddhist leaders from Asia. Third, the visiting Buddhist monks, nuns, and scholars from Asia would focus their time and efforts on the larger and influential U.S. audiences rather than those in Canada. And their influence occurred during a longer period as the U.S. had become an independent country earlier than Canada as noted in the first reason.

Living Buddhism, as practiced by ordinary people, arrived on the West Coast of Canada with Chinese and Japanese immigrants who brought it as their religion. As Buddhists, they built temples, which served as religious and cultural centres as they began their new lives in the new land. In Canada, Buddhism spread predominantly across its three major provinces: British Columbia (BC); Ontario (ON); and Quebec (QC). This is not to say that

---

47. Johanna Read (2020). *When did Canada become a country?* https://www.rd.com/article/when-did-canada-become-a-country/

48. Dalstrom. H.A. (n.d.). *Nebraska State, United States*. https://www.britannica.com/place/Nebraska-state

other Canadian regions lacked the presence of Buddhism; it is just that these three provinces have the largest number of Buddhists. We will now take an overview of the temporal and spatial development of "living" Buddhism in these three provinces.

British Columbia

"Living" Buddhism had slowly advanced in Canada through four means: increased immigration by Buddhists, increase in their religious institutions, new converts to Buddhism, and a Canadian legislation called the Multiculturalism Act enacted in 1988. Chinese and Japanese immigrants brought "living" Buddhism to Canada in the second half of the 19th century. They established temples, mostly on the West Coast, serving as important centres of their religious and community life.

This early period was difficult. For example, wary of raising racial tensions, early Shin (or Jodo Shinshu) Buddhists in BC addressed this concern by "Christianizing" their Buddhist practice by identifying their temples as "churches" with pews in their worship hall. They also held Sunday schools and Sunday services that included the singing of hymnals.[49] These were all customs and practices not found in their ancestorial land, Japan. Further, Shin Buddhists put the construction of their Steveston Buddhist Church on hold because of their fear that Anglo-Canadians may perceive Buddhism as representing Japanese nationalism. In 1927, two Christian pastors opposed Buddhist propagation by Nishi Hongwanji Minister Gijin Taga in Kelowna. However, the Japanese Canadian Buddhists succeeded in persevering and establishing a Buddhist temple there in 1933.[50] Given this environment that discouraged the

Welcome Party for Rev. Nishimoto with Dharma School Students and YBA (Young Buddhist Association) in 1920.

Photo courtesy of the Vancouver Buddhist Temple

---

49. Crowe Paul, "Dharma on the move: Vancouver Buddhist Communities and Multiculturalism" in *Flowers on the Rock: Global and local Buddhisms in Canada* edited by Harding, J.S., Hori, V.S and Soucy, A. (McGill-Queen's University Press, 2014)

50. Ama Michihiro, "Flying sparks: Dissension among the early Shin Buddhists in Canada" in *Flowers on the Rock: Global and Local Buddhism in Canada* edited by Harding. J, Hori, V.S. and Soucy, A. McGill-Queen's University Press (2014)

presence of Buddhism, the religious expressions of Chinese immigrants had such a low profile that there is virtually no data on the number and nature of their institutions before World War II. (See Crowe in footnote 49) Japanese and Chinese Canadians contributed to "living" Buddhism differently. The Japanese were organized and the headquarters of the various Buddhist denominations in Japan sent professional priests as missionaries to Canada. In 1905, the Buddhist Mission of North America (BMNA), established in San Francisco in 1898, extended its services to Japanese Buddhists living in Vancouver. This led to the formation of the Honpa Canada Buddhist Mission (HCBM) and the construction of temples in Vancouver, Maple Ridge, Fairview, Steveston, New Westminster, Royston (Vancouver Island) and Raymond (Alberta).[51] In 1904, Japanese Buddhists met in Vancouver to discuss the possibility of building a temple there. At their request, the Nishi Hongwanji headquarters in Kyoto sent a minister named Senju Sasaki to Vancouver in 1905. In 1906, the Shin Buddhists formed a Young Men's Buddhist Association.

Photo courtesy of the JCCC Archives

Rev. Senju and Tomie Sasaki, Vancouver Buddhist Church. First Jodo Shinshu priest in Canada. 1905.

It is speculated that prior to 1970, there were only two major Chinese temples in Canada, which were both located in the oldest Chinatown in Canada, in Victoria, BC. Both folk temples had Buddhist images and objects incorporated in the temple liturgies. The first was Tam Kung temple located in a single-story house rented by a Hakka society and officially dedicated on 21 January 1876. The second temple, Laat Sing Kung temple, was established in 1885 on the top floor of the Chinese Consolidated Benevolent Association. More Chinese temples followed as Chinese immigration increased in Canada. (See Crowe in footnote 49) In 1881, a building called Lytton Joss House was built in Lytton, BC, for Chinese immigrants. Quan Yin (the Goddess of Mercy) and Shen Nong (the God of Agriculture) were two two deities honored at the temple. As Chinese folk temples cannot be separated from Buddhist images and liturgy, this temple can also be considered one of the earliest Chinese Buddhist temples in BC.[52]

In more recent time, Venerable Lianci established the Lotus Light Temple in Vancouver in 1996 at the urging of Lu Shengyen, the head of the True Buddha school in Taiwan. It is one of the more than forty True Buddha

---

51. Please see above.

52. Lytton Chinese History Museum (2022). Retrieved https://lyttonchinesehistorymuseum.com/pages/mission]

school temples across the world of which ten are in Canada.

In 1983, Venerable Hsuan Hua inaugurated the Gold Buddha Monastery in Vancouver. In 1999, the Ling Yen Mountain Temple was established in Richmond, BC. It is linked to a monastery of the same name in Taiwan.[53] In 2006, the Dharma Drum Mountain Vancouver Centre was established.

The number of non-Chinese Buddhists has increased in recent years. They tend to be more interested in practicing meditation and learning Buddhist philosophy in English as compared to their Chinese counterparts who are drawn to rituals at the same temples. The rise of non-Asian participation can be seen, for example, in the Shin Buddhist temples. There have been several Caucasian priests leading their communities.

Also, in the early days of the Gold Buddha monastery in Vancouver, primarily non-Asian Americans took on leadership roles at the temple. In 1983, two young Caucasian monks, Venerable Heng Sure and Venerable Heng Chau, served the mostly Cantonese immigrant membership. Similarly at the Tung Lin Kok Yuen Canada Society Temple in Vancouver, a Caucasian monk serves as its priest.[54]

As discussed here, the earliest Buddhist activities occurred on the West Coast in British Columbia. Although today Ontario has the largest number of Buddhists in Canada, it was British Columbia where living Buddhism first took root.

Ontario

The first Buddhist temple in Toronto was the Toronto Buddhist Church founded in the late 1940s by Japanese Canadians who were forced by the Canadian government to resettle in Eastern Canada from their wartime internment camps in British Columbia from 1941 to 1945.[55] A Canadian born Caucasian, Leslie George Dawson, who was trained as a Theravada monk in the late 1950s in Burma, founded the first non-Asian Buddhist group called the Dharma Center of Canada in Toronto in 1966. Then in 1967, the Canadian Immigration Act removed specific country restrictions and introduced points systems to determine immigration eligibility. This made it easier for Buddhist immigrants from Sri Lanka, Burma, Hong Kong, Korea, and India to settle down in the Toronto area in increasing numbers in the years that followed.

---

53. Please see Crowe (2014).

54. Please see Crowe (2014).

55. McLellan Janet, "Buddhism in Greater Toronto area: the politics of recognition" in *Buddhism in Canada* edited by Bruce Matthews. (Routledge, 2004)

In 1971, a group of two hundred twenty-eight Tibetan Buddhists became the first non-European refugees to be accepted into Canada. They were settled in four provinces across eleven localities in the country; Lindsay in Ontario was one of them. In the 1970s and 80s, more Tibetan monks arrived in Toronto through the family member sponsorships, and some student groups requested permanent teachers from an Indian Buddhist monastery.[56]

By early 1970s, several Korean, Chinese, Burmese and Sri Lankan temples were established in the Greater Toronto area. Of all the Canadian provinces, Ontario has the highest number of Buddhists. The 2001 Census revealed that 43 percent of Canada's Buddhists live in Ontario, 29 percent in BC, and 14 percent in Quebec.[57] Over 75 percent of Ontario's Buddhists live in the Greater Toronto area, and over 80 percent of Ontario's Buddhists are new Canadians.[58] The Vietnamese, the Lao, the Khmer (Cambodians), the Sri Lankans, and the Chinese from Vietnam, Hong Kong and mainland China form the bulk of the new arrivals in Ontario. Today, temples and meditation centres of Mahayana, Theravada, and Vajrayana traditions from a large number of regions of Asia are dispersed across Ontario. As it is the economic and financial powerhouse of the country, the province will continue to attract a significant proportion of Buddhist immigrants.

Quebec

Although Quebec has Buddhists of various traditions, it sets the scene for Vietnamese Buddhist immigration, a relative latecomer to Canada as compared to the Chinese and Japanese arrivals. Vietnamese Buddhists headed for Quebec because the Vietnam was once a French colony and Quebec is a French speaking province. The Vietnamese started arriving in Quebec as students in the 1950s, but it was in 1975 and later that Canada saw more Vietnamese arriving as refugees as the Communist government restructured Vietnamese society.[59]

Canada took over 10 percent of the two million refugees called "Boat People," mostly Vietnamese but also including Laotians and Cambodians. These arrivals in the late 1970s and early '80s laid the foundation for the for-

---

56. Please see McLellan above

57. CBC News (2021). *Buddhism: Facts & Figures.* https://www.cbc.ca/news2/background/religion/fact-buddhism.html

58. Koppedrayer Kay & Fenn, Mavis. L, "Buddhist diversity in Ontario" in *Buddhism in Canada* edited by Bruce Matthews. (Routledge, 2004)

59. Soucy Alexander, "Thay Pho Tinh: A Vietnamese nun's struggles in Canada" in *Flowers on the Rock: Global and Local Buddhism in Canada*, edited by Harding. J, Hori, V.S. and Soucy, A. (McGill-Queen's University Press, 2014)

mation of religious associations. Eventually, these communities sponsored monks to arrive and reside in the temples built by them. After training, some monks formed their own temples by taking their set of followers with them. By 2014, this cumulative process had snowballed into the presence of fifty-five Vietnamese temples across Canada. This did not include the meditation groups started by a Vietnamese monk, the late Thich Nhat Hanh, which catered mostly to non-Vietnamese.[60]

The first Vietnamese temple in Canada, the Lien Hoa Temple in Brossard QC, and the Tam Bao Temple in Harrington QC, both acted as the principal sources from which the various temples were established across the country. They also contributed to the establishment of the Union of Vietnamese Buddhist Churches in Canada (UVBCC) and its subsequent operations. Thay Pho Tinh, the first nun to lead a Buddhist institution in Canada, and her uncle, Thich Thien Nghi, were two of the earliest monastics in Canada. They played vital roles in the establishment of UVBCC and the Tam Bao Temple.

One of the reasons behind the proliferation of Vietnamese temples is attributed to the refusal of trainee monks arriving from Vietnam to accept the status of female authority of Thay Pho Tinh at the Tam Bao Temple. Many of these trainee monks left and started their own temples.[61] However, she was supported by Thich Thien Nghi, who stood steadfast on gender equality in Canada and refused to adopt the unequal status between the monks and nuns traditionally found in Vietnam. The gallant efforts by these two leaders to maintain their progressive position pushed the conservative monks to set out on their own, thus, ironically contributing to the increase in the number of Vietnamese temples in Canada.

Multiculturalism Act, 1988 and Living Buddhism

In 2005, the Richmond BC based Ling Yen Mountain Temple approached the Richmond City Council for zoning permit to construct a thirty-meter-tall, gilded Buddha statue. If approved, it would have become the highest structure in the Richmond Municipality. However, the permit was denied due partly to the opposition of the local non-Buddhist residents and the media. Eventually the temple and the local community arrived at a consensus to approve the building of the statue as its height was reduced and its site was moved further away from the highway.

---

60. Please see above.

61. Please see above.

Despite strong opposition, the Buddhist community elected to push forward with its project plans. This proved to be a far cry from the past when the community had to hide their religious institutions from the public glare.[62] This example demonstrates the Buddhist community's religious assertion, empowered in part by the rights granted by Canada's Multiculturalism Act, 1988. The Multiculturalism Act has contributed significantly to the presence of Living Buddhism to reach a higher level and is expected to continue to facilitate its growth in Canada.

Important Events in Canadian Buddhist History

Having painted an overview of how Buddhism developed in Canada, we wish to conclude this chapter by listing some of the important historical events that have shaped the overall character of Buddhism in Canada. For important events shaping each of the many Buddhist traditions, please refer to their respective histories.

1788: The first Chinese land at Nootka Sound, British Columbia.[63] However, there is no record of religious activity.

1876: Tam Kung temple, located in a single storey house rented by a Hakka society, was officially dedicated on 21st January 1876 in Victoria, BC.[64]

1881: Chinese temple established at Lytton Joss House in Lytton, BC.

1885: Laat Sing Kung shrine installed on the top floor of the Chinese Consolidated Benevolent Association in Victoria, BC.

1905: the Buddhist Mission of North America (BMNA), which began in San Francisco in 1898, extends its services to Japanese residents in Vancouver.[65]

1946: The Toronto Buddhist Church is established at 918 Bathurst Street, which was later renamed "Toronto Buddhist Temple" and moved to Sheppard Avenue, North Toronto in early 2000s.[66]

1949: The Hamilton and Thunder Bay Buddhist temples (both Jodo Shinshu) are established in Toronto.[67]

1965: Anagarika Dhammadinna (Anna Burian), a pioneer of Theravada Buddhism in Western Canada, returns to Canada after her travels to

---

62. See Crowe (2014).

63. See above.

64. See above.

65. See Michihiro Ama above.

66. A significant part of the chronology has been extracted from Sugunasiri above.

67. See Koppedrayer & Fenn (2004).

India and Sri Lanka to settle in Nelson, British Columbia.[68]

1966: Namgyal Rinpoche (formerly Leslie George Dawson, mentioned earlier) establishes the Dharma Centre of Canada in Kinmount, Ontario just outside Toronto.

1967: Chinese Buddhist monk Ven. Sing Hung Fa Shih establishes the Sau Fau Temple at 100 Southhill Road, Don Mills, Ontario.

1968: Buddhist Association of Canada formed by Ven. Lok To, Ven. Shing Cheung and Ven. Sing Hung.[69] Taiwan based businessman C.C. Lu provides financial support to establish Vancouver's oldest active Chinese Buddhist temple, the Universal Buddhist Temple in Chinatown. It was later moved to 49th Ave. at Fraser Street.

1970: Ven. Chogyam Trungpa establishes the earliest Tibetan Centre, the Toronto Dharmadhatu in Toronto.

1975: Montreal Zen Centre is set up by Philip Kapleau. Albert Low becomes its Spiritual Director in 1985.

1976: Chan Nhu, the first Vietnamese Buddhist group, is formed, and the first Vietnamese Buddhist Temple, the Lien Hoa Temple, is established in Brossard, Quebec.[70]

1978: Ven. Dr. Walpola Piyananda starts the first Sinhala Buddhist Theravada centre in Toronto named, the Toronto Mahavira Dhamma School.[71]

Late 1970s: Korean monk Samu Sunim establishes a Zen Buddhist temple at 46 Gwynne Avenue, Toronto, ten years after arriving in Montreal.

1981: Gaden Choling Tibetan Temple headed by Zasep Tulku Rinpoche is established. The Toronto Buddhist Federation (which later became the Buddhist Federation of Toronto) holds a Vesak Day celebration for the first time in Toronto at 252 Bloor Street.

1983: Renowned Canadian Buddhist scholar and practitioner Dr. Suwanda H.J. Sugunasiri is appointed by Order-in-Council to the Ontario Advisory Council on Multi-culturalism and Citizenship. Master Hsuan

---

68. Fenn Mavis L, "Dhammadinna and Jayanta" in *Flowers on the Rock: Global and local Buddhisms in Canada* edited by Harding, J.S., Hori, V.S and Soucy, A. (McGill-Queen's University Press, 2014).

69. History of the Buddhist Association of Canada Cham Shan Temple (2010) http://en.chamshantemple.org/messages/aboutus/index.php?channelId=8&sectionId=109&itemId=87&attachId=0&langCd=EN

70. Confirmed by a personal telephone conversation on 3rd April 2021 between author Kasbekar and Chen Te, the monk at the temple.

71. Barua, Mitra D, *Teaching Buddhism to children: The evolving Sri Lankan Buddhist tradition in multi-cultural Toronto*. In Flowers on the Rock: Global and Local Buddhism in Canada-Edited by Harding. J, Hori, V.S. and Soucy, A. (McGill-Queen's University Press. 2014).

Hua facilitates the opening of Gold Buddha Monastery on Gore Street, Vancouver.

1985: Buddhist Council of Canada comes into being with Professor Stanley Fefferman, of York University and a member of the Dharmadhatu, as its first President. The Canadian Broadcasting Corporation covers Vesak 1985 from coast to coast under its Open House programme.

1989: The first and the only Congress of the Buddhist Council of Canada is held in Toronto.

1992: The Mississauga West End Dhamma School (the largest Buddhist school for children in North America) is founded in Ontario.[72]

1988: The Union of Vietnamese Buddhist Churches in Canada (UVBCC) is formed.

2004: University of British Columbia, University of Toronto and Simon Fraser University confer Honourary Doctorates to the Dalai Lama, the same year he delivers the Kalachakra Initiation in Toronto.

2005: Vesak celebrated at Queens Park, Toronto under the auspices of the Nalanda College of Buddhist Studies celebrating "100 years of Buddhism in Canada". As another event for celebrating "100 years of Buddhism in Canada", a Paritta (spirit) chanting ceremony is held at the Ontario Institute for Studies in Education (the first time such a ceremony is held in Canada). Professor Sugunasiri starts the *Canadian Journal of Buddhist Studies*.

2006: Dalai Lama granted Honourary Citizenship of Canada during his Vancouver visit. Dharma Drum Mountain Vancouver Centre opens in Vancouver

2010: The Jade Buddha, made of BC jade, returns to Canada for a cross-country tour.

2012: Ven. Bhante Saranapala organizes Unity Vesak held in North Toronto bringing diverse Buddhist communities together.

2013 (July-August): Buddhist Council of Canada organizes *Windows to Buddhism in the Academy*, a display of books on Buddhism available at Roberts Library, University of Toronto.

2014: The number of Vietnamese Buddhist temples across Canada reaches fifty-five. This number does not include Thich Nhat Hanh's meditation groups.[73] Vesak 2014 is organized by three temples in Mississauga with additional twenty-seven temples around Toronto and societies around the Greater Toronto Area. The Maitreya Loving Kindness Tour

---

72. Please see Barua (2014).

73. Please see Soucy Alexander, "Thay Pho Tinh: A Vietnamese Nun's struggles in Canada" above.

of Buddhist relics makes multiple stops in Canada. (10th October): MPP Damerla organizes the Buddhism Heritage Day at the Ontario Legislature attended by one hundred fifty Buddhists. UBC launches The Robert H.N. Ho Family Foundation Program in Buddhism and Contemporary Society.

2016: Monks from a Toronto Vajrayana centre take two weeks creating a sand mandala at the Canadian National Exhibition. The University of Toronto launches The Robert H.N. Ho Family Foundation Centre for Buddhist Studies on its St. George campus.

2017: The first Canadian Buddhist Literary Festival takes place as part of the Word on the Street Literary Festival in Toronto. The Tenth Global Conference On Buddhism takes place in Toronto that year too.

2018: The World Parliament of Religions is held in Toronto, with multiple events by Buddhist teachers and communities.

2021: The 17th Sakyadhita International Conference On Buddhist Women takes place online, with involvement from Sakyadhita Canada.

2022: The second Canadian Buddhist Literary Festival takes place online, hosted by Emmanuel College at the University of Toronto.

Part Two

Basic Teachings and Practices with Humour and Light-hearted Stories

6 Four Noble Truths

Four Noble Truths and the Greedy Dog

AMONG THE BUDDHA'S TEACHINGS, the most basic and important are the Four Noble Truths. That is the reason why they were the topic of the Buddha's first sermon, which, if you recall, he gave to the five monks.

And we are told that soon after Buddha's sermon ended, all five of the monks had attained Awakening. So, the Four Noble Truths were the very teaching that led to the Awakening of his first disciples. This was significant because it proved that his teaching was effective not only for himself but for other people as well.

The Four Noble Truths also give us the bird's-eye view or the road map of the Buddha's overall teachings. In other words, it's a great place to start. The Four Noble Truths are usually expressed as follows:
- The first truth of suffering
- The second truth of the cause of suffering
- The third truth of cessation
- The fourth truth of the path

However, I would like to restate these truths in ways that are easier to understand:
- First truth: We all experience suffering.
- Second truth: The cause of our suffering lies in our attachments.
- Third truth: Our suffering ceases when Awakening is realized.
- Fourth truth: There is the Eightfold Noble Path for realizing Awakening.

Now, let us see if we can make the Four Noble Truths, especially the first two, more understandable. I find that stories are very effective for that. There are many traditional Buddhist stories, but I shall utilize a story that many of you are more familiar with.[74] Plus, the story is in keeping with the tone of this book to be as lighthearted and humourous as possible.

---

74. Buddhism spread across vast areas to become a world religion because it succeeded in adapting ideas and stories which were originally not "Buddhist" but were familiar to the new people in the new culture.

Aesop's fable of "The Greedy Dog"

The famous Aesop's fable of "The Greedy Dog" is a great way to understand the Four Noble Truths. Once upon a time, a hungry old dog saw a puppy carrying a juicy bone in its mouth. Greedy for the puppy's treat, the old dog barked and growled until the poor puppy got scared, dropped the bone, and ran away. The old dog carried off the juicy bone in its mouth and looked around to find a quiet place to eat it.

On his way to a quiet place, he walked over a bridge, and as he looked over its side, he saw *another* dog with a bone in its mouth. Not realizing that the other dog he saw was actually him reflected in the water, he became greedy for *another* bone and barked at the other dog. As he did, "splash" went his own bone as it fell into the river, leaving the dog with no bone, hungry once again. No doubt, this greedy dog was suffering.

First truth:
We all experience suffering

Buddhism is sometimes accused of being too "pessimistic" precisely because there is much talk about suffering, as is seen here. But isn't it the role of any true religion to face up to and overcome suffering? The overall purpose of Buddhism has been "to *eliminate* or *reduce* suffering and to bring about true happiness."

The first of the Four Noble Truths states, "We all experience suffering." Isn't that the truth! Even teenagers can agree with this, for while there is much happiness in life, there is also much suffering.

The Buddha specified eight kinds of suffering, which are:
1. birth
2. aging
3. illness
4. death
5. having to meet up with people and situations we don't like
6. having to separate from people and situations we like
7. not getting what we want
8. being attached to the five physical-psychological components that make up our experience

Now, let us look at the each of these sufferings. As we do this, you might ask, "Why is birth a form of suffering?" After all, when a baby is born the family and friends all celebrate the arrival of new life. The answer to this requires more space, so we will come back to this later. (See pp. 141) Having so said, please begin thinking why "birth" is considered suffering in Buddhism.

Compared to birth, it is easy to see how aging, illness and death are considered suffering. Remember, it was seeing an old person, a sick person and a deceased person that shocked and pained the prince who later became the Buddha. These experiences motivated him to leave his family and comfortable life to seek the spiritual path.

As for the fifth suffering of "having to face people and situations we don't like," we saw a perfect example of it with in the story of the Greedy Dog. There the puppy experienced this suffering when he faced the greedy dog that frightened him and ended up taking his bone. In our lives, examples of this fifth suffering include having to do that dreaded homework, losing a close sports match, and having to be in the same class or team with people we don't like or whom we might even hate. What are other examples of this kind of suffering that you can think of?

The sixth suffering of "having to separate from people and situations we like" also takes place often in our lives. For example, it includes having to say goodbye to our loved ones. We have done that when our grandparents passed away or when we parted ways from our girlfriend or boyfriend when we still cared for him or her. Also, some of us had to leave a school or neighbourhood that we loved on account of our family moving far away.

Next, the dog's plight applies to the seventh suffering, "not getting what we want." The puppy was about to enjoy the bone, but the big, greedy dog came to take it away by force. There was nothing the puppy could do, so he was left "without what he wanted."

Finally, let us look at the eighth suffering, that of "attachment to the five physical-psychological functions (or aggregates)." This one is a bit harder to understand for it looks at suffering from a more objective and psychological perspective.

These five functions that make up our experiences are the 1) body and five senses, 2) feelings, 3) thoughts, 4) intention, and 5) consciousness. According to the Buddha, we suffer because our five functions are tainted by our attachment or G.A.S. (greed, anger/hatred and stupidity).

For example, when the greedy dog saw and smelled the juicy bone through his *senses* of sight and smell, it was followed by pleasant *feelings* about the bone, which generated a desire for it. This feeling then led to his *thoughts* of determining that he could easily overpower the tiny puppy in order to snatch its bone. And then he raised the *intention* of taking it away from the puppy. Finally, the fifth function, *consciousness*, includes the decision he made to take the bone away based on his awareness of the previous four functions.[75]

It was the self-centred attachments of greed and stupidity (two of G.A.S.) that led to the greedy dog wanting the bone (feelings), knowing that he could overpower the puppy (thoughts), then wanting to scare and snatch away the bone from the puppy (intention), and finally making the decision (consciousness). While the greedy dog was experiencing all this, he was not at all at peace or happy; his greed and aggressive actions made him very anxious and agitated.

Certainly, he ended up suffering a lot when he dropped the bone into the river. He suffered a great deal because he became greatly agitated, frustrated and regretful.

We must remember that it wasn't only the greedy dog that suffered, for the poor puppy also suffered. The puppy became terrified and upset when the greedy dog growled at him and stole the bone the puppy had looked forward to chewing. This goes to show that our action impacts not only our own happiness but also that of others.

Second truth:
The cause of our suffering lies in our attachment or clinging

As we look at the second of the Four Noble Truths, I wish to begin with a well-known American Buddhist joke that was mentioned earlier.
A: Why couldn't the Buddha vacuum clean under the sofa?
B: I don't know.
A: Well, it's because the Buddha had no attachments!

Allow me to explain even if you got it. As an Awakened person, the Buddha no longer has any attachments or G.A.S. (greed, anger/hatred and stupidity). At the same time, "attachments" also refer to the gadgets that are attached to the end of the vacuum cleaner for reaching narrow spaces such as under a sofa. That is why the Buddha had no *attachments* to get to the narrow space! I hope you got it.

This second truth emphasizes the fact that our suffering is caused by G.A.S. This was obvious in the case of the greedy dog, for

---

75. I am explaining this complex teaching of "attachment to the five physical-psychological functions (or aggregates)" in ways that are easier to understand for our readers.

it was because of his greed and stupidity that he suffered the loss of his bone. His greed also brought great suffering and misery to the puppy.

In the case of Prince Siddhartha, before he became the Buddha, he experienced extreme suffering upon witnessing a dead person. And his pain and suffering were due to his desire (or greed) to want to live, or in his own words, due to his "craving for existence." And this was compounded by his ignorance (or stupidity) about the truth of impermanence, that is, that everything including our body changes and eventually ceases to exist.

Now, we can certainly empathize with Prince Siddhartha, because everyone desires to live a long time and to be in good health. However, no matter how common and universal the thirst for life is, it is still *greed*, nevertheless. This truth (that desire to live is, indeed, greed) discovered by the Buddha will probably be hard to swallow for many of us.

It certainly was for me, when I was rudely awakened in my sophomore year in high school that we all have to die. I vividly recall feeling that it was unfair, and that it wasn't how it was supposed to be. And the Buddhist teaching wasn't much of a consolation *initially* when it reminded me that my discomfort with death was due to my greed and attachment to life.

However, the teaching has since helped me to see that the roots of my suffering regarding death lie within *myself*. It was my greed and stupidity (or ignorance) that were preventing me from having the wisdom to see and live in accord with the truth: everything changes and comes to an end, including my body.

So, my suffering was due to my failure to develop the wisdom or awaken to truth. This may differ a bit from Christianity, where suffering stems from our "sin," due to our failure to keep our promise or covenant with God. Buddhism values wisdom to see truth, while it seems to me that Christianity values humans' relationship to God. However, in the end, the values of the two religions can be seen to be similar, since God for Christians is truth, and wisdom for Buddhists is to awaken to truth.

Third truth:
Our suffering ceases when Awakening is realized

Now, let's move to the third truth, which states that our suffering ceases when Awakening is realized. Awakening is the state realized by the Buddha under the Bodhi tree and is also known as "nirvana."

"Nirvana" literally means "blown out." So, it is the state when the fire of attachments or G.A.S. has been blown out. You can now find "nirvana" in your dictionary as an *English* word and it has come to mean "extreme happiness, bliss, freedom and/or liberation."

In the 1980s and 1990s, there was, as previously mentioned, an internationally famous American rock band called "Nirvana." When asked why they settled on that name for his band, the singer and guitarist Kurt Cobain answered that he "wanted a name that was kind of beautiful or nice and pretty instead of a mean, raunchy punk name...." In that same article of the interview, Nirvana is described as "transformed state of personality characterized by compassion, peace, deep spiritual joy and an absence of negative mental states and emotions such as doubt, worry, anxiety and fear."[76]

To better understand this state of Awakening or nirvana, I wish to share another well-known Buddhist joke.

A Buddhist monk wanted a hot dog, so he walked over to a hot dog vendor on a busy street corner. The vender asked, "What would you like, sir?" The monk answered, "Make me *one* with *everything*!"

To make sure you got it, let me explain. The conventional meaning is that he wanted one hot dog with all the condiments, which include mustard, ketchup, diced onion, pickle relish, and sauerkraut: in other words, "make me *one* [hot dog] *with everything* [on it]."

But the deeper meaning points to a religious experience wherein a person feels at "unity with" or "one with" other people, nature and the universe ("everything"), associated with the state of Awakening; so, in other words, "*make me one* with everything."

The Buddha experienced a profound realization in which he no longer saw himself as being separate and alone but connected to everything around him as in our metaphor of Indra's Net of Gems. Within this experience of interconnectedness, the Buddha now saw clearly 1) the nature of suffering, 2) the cause of suffering, and 3) the path to overcoming suffering. This Awakening revealed that change had to come from within himself.

Now here comes the follow up to the joke about the monk and a hot dog, which directly illustrates the present topic. Well, after getting the hot dog, the monk gives the vendor a $20 bill, but even though a minute passed, he did not get the change back.

The monk waited patiently for a while but when it was not forthcoming, the monk became a bit flustered and finally asked, "Well, where is my change?" The vendor squarely faced the monk and replied with confidence, "Sir, the *change* must come from *within you*," as he pointed his index

---

76. Briony Edwards, "Nirvana: Everything you need to know." https://www.loudersound.com/features/nirvana-everything-you-need-to-know

finger toward the Buddhist monk!

The monk wanted "change" as *in money*, but the vendor switched the meaning of "change" to mean *transforming* the mind or Awakening. And the joke becomes funnier since the roles are reversed. It should be the monk telling the vendor. However, it is the hot dog vendor telling the monk what the monk should already know: Awakening involves *change* in the way we see things in accordance with truth. And it is this change that leads to the gem within each of us to shine forth!

Fourth truth:
There is the Eightfold Noble Path for realizing Awakening

This Awakening or nirvana is realized by practicing the fourth truth. This road map is called the Eightfold Noble Path. What are the eight? They are:
1. Right View
2. Right Intention
3. Right Speech
4. Right Conduct
5. Right Livelihood
6. Right Effort
7. Right Mindfulness
8. Right Concentration or Meditation

We shall in subsequent chapters explore each of these for they deserve to be discussed in greater depth. (See Chapter 7) For now, the list gives us a sense of what is required in order to attain Awakening.

So, between the fourth and the third truths, there also exists a cause-and-effect relationship. By practicing the Eightfold Noble Path (the fourth truth) one can achieve nirvana or Awakening (the third truth), when suffering ends or is overcome.

For those who have a hard time remembering all eight parts of the Eightfold Noble Path, I'd like to share a tip that one of my teachers taught us for remembering them. He said to think of a German name, Mr. V.I. SCLEMM (pronounced "Shlem"); for example, "V" stands for "View" and "I" stands for "Intention" and so on! It's certainly helped *me* to remember the eight. I hope that it can help you as well.

Summarizing the Four Noble Truths

So, the Four Noble Truths are comprised of two sets of cause-and-effect relationships. The second truth is the *cause* of the first truth, and the fourth truth is the *cause* of the third truth. And, most importantly, when the third truth (Awakening) is attained, the first truth (suffering) ceases.

When we evaluate the Four Noble Truths, they are quite *scientific* in nature. They do not require us to believe in something that we cannot experience in our lives. They tell us that we experience suffering, and then proceed to tell us what the causes are.

And then they show us how we can think, speak, and act in the right way; this is Karma. Karma means "our *action* in how we act, speak and think" (Three Actions). Its original meaning was not "fate," although it has unfortunately come to be understood that way today. So, if our Karma or action is in keeping with the Four Noble Truths, we are able to reduce our suffering as well as that of others.

Now, let's see if we can summarize the Four Noble Truths by taking a final look at the greedy dog. Well, some of you may be saying to yourselves, "What a stupid, greedy dog!" But are we so different? Don't we sometimes find ourselves in the same situation? Aren't we swept away by our greed for more and more things?

As a result, we see some of our parents being overburdened with huge debts and overtime work that put undue pressure on them and on their relationships with other people, including you. So, they end up not having enough time to spend with you and the other family members, with their friends, and with each other. Not having enough time for each other, some couples grow distant and their relationships end up in divorce. Or the stressful life can take a toll on the mind and body, leading to psychological and physical problems.

We could blame our greed on how our consumer-oriented society that forces us to spend-and-spend and buy-and-buy. Certainly, we have one of the richest societies in the history of humankind, where some middle-class people are able to live in four-bedroom homes with three-car garages. And many of these houses are located miles away from places of work, school, and shopping, requiring multiple cars and a lot of gasoline. Our lifestyle leads us to spend and consume enormously. And if we are not careful, it can bury us under the weight of our greed. One such serious outcome is the devastating effects of climate change.

But to travel the Buddhist path means to be self-directed, not simply to blame others or the economic system, and not to feel victimized. We can choose our own lifestyle as well as help to change the system to encourage a lifestyle of less consumption. We can do that in the spirit of engaged Buddhism, in which we are inspired to take the teachings from the personal level and apply them to the societal level.

And, of course, we can and we should on a personal level work to control our G.A.S. We could let our greed, anger/hatred and stupidity get out of control, like the greedy dog, and suffer. The greedy dog should not have acted out on his greed to take the bone away from the puppy.

Or we can apply the Four Noble Truths to our lives, to see the various temptations in our lives, and take appropriate measures, as found in the Eightfold Noble Path. This is why the Buddha stressed the Four Noble Truths, as the following scriptural passage indicates:

> All those who are seeking Awakening must understand the Four Noble Truths. Without understanding these, they will wander about interminably in the bewildering maze of life's illusions. Those who understand these Four Noble Truths are called "the people who have acquired the eyes of Awakening." (*Ithivuttaka*)

Whether we suffer or not is up to each of us. This idea is expressed in a somewhat humourous line, "Suffering is optional," which has become quite a popular phrase found in books and on television.

Actually, I first came across these words among the graffiti on a wall in, of all places, a public restroom! I could not help blurting out laughing when I found such a statement of truth on a restroom wall. It read:

"Suffering is optional!"

Now, I have since added "Difficulties are inevitable," so as to read, "Difficulties are inevitable, but suffering is optional!" We all know that difficulties are inevitable in life, but by practicing the Four Noble Truths they do not necessarily have to become *my* suffering, thus, "suffering is optional." So, suffering is up to you.

A lesson to be learned from the Four Noble Truths

We wish to conclude with a very important lesson we can learn from the Four Noble Truths, and that is this: by learning to let go or reduce our G.A.S., we can reduce our suffering for ourselves and for others. This is an optimistic message even though we, as persons leading ordinary lives in the modern world, would not be able to *completely* let go or eliminate G.A.S. as did the Buddha.

Nevertheless, by putting the Four Noble Truths into practice, there will be a real difference in our lives. This difference will become clear the more we put them into action in our daily lives.

In this regard, we should not misunderstand the aim of the Four Noble Truths. Just because the first truth has to do with suffering, it does not mean that it's the most important or is the conclusion. Instead, the Four Noble

Truths *conclude* with Awakening (the third truth) or nirvana, which is none other than "ultimate happiness, bliss, freedom and/or liberation" and the path to it.

This misunderstanding often becomes the basis for many people, especially those of other religions, who see Buddhism to be overly negative and pessimistic. However, if the critics were correct, Buddhism would not have inspired and brought happiness to millions of people for twenty-six centuries. Such true happiness is also reflected in the peaceful smiles and faces on the artistic images of the Buddhas and Bodhisattvas!

7 Karma and the Eightfold Noble Path

A Stolen Car

LET'S BEGIN with a humourous episode between a Buddhist named Stephen, a relative newcomer to Buddhism, and his Buddhist priest.

> STEPHEN: Can you bless my new car?
> BUDDHIST PRIEST: What benefits do you hope to get from a blessing?
> STEPHEN: I want nothing bad to happen to my brand-new car.
> BUDDHIST PRIEST: We don't usually do blessings since they go against our teachings, but if you really insist, I shall do it as a pastoral service to give you peace of mind.
> (*A few weeks later, Stephen returns, really upset, to tell the priest that the car was stolen.*)
> STEPHEN: Reverend, my car was stolen yesterday! I feel that your blessing didn't work.
> BUDDHIST PRIEST: I'm very sorry to hear that, but that blessing doesn't work for stolen cars; it works only for preventing the car from getting into an accident!

This episode is meant to point out the folly of relying on religion to prevent bad things from happening to us. Buddhism, or any religion for that matter, cannot control or determine what happens to us. What is important in Buddhism is not *what happens* to us but how we *experience* life. So, in this case, religion cannot prevent the car from being stolen or also from getting into a car accident but can help us mentally and spiritually to deal better with the misfortunes of life.

And how we experience our lives depends on the quality of the jewel of wisdom within ourselves. This wisdom can also be expressed as "understanding," "view," or "insight." Whatever we call it, Buddhism encourages us to cultivate it.

What Karma Is Not

Before moving on to discuss the ways of cultivating the jewel of wisdom within, we would like to discuss the teaching of Karma. It is a well-known word but often highly *misunderstood* and *misused*. Let's use the example of the stolen car.

A wrong use of the word is to say that it was Stephen's Karma that the car was stolen, meaning that the theft of the car was due to "fate" or "predestination." So, based on this way of thinking, no matter how much Stephen had taken steps to secure his car by always locking it and parking in safe places, his car was "fated" or "predetermined" to be stolen.

Another wrong understanding of Karma is to think that Stephen was being punished for something "bad" he had done recently. Actually, a few days before his car was stolen, Stephen was so upset over his team's loss in overtime in an important basketball match that he took out his frustration on others. He purposely stepped on a bug on the sidewalk and yelled at the family dog! However, these did not *directly cause* Stephen's car from being stolen. The stolen car was not a punishment for his bad behaviour.

In my understanding of Buddhism, there are two basic categories of cause and effect: 1) objective conditions and 2) personal Karma. Stephen getting his car stolen was a result of the first category but not the second. The objective conditions point to a myriad of circumstances that contributed to the car being stolen.

These include the fact that Stephen's car matched perfectly what the burglar was looking for, and the burglar happened to have exactly the right tools for disarming the alarm system on Stephen's car. So, the causes leading to Stephen's car getting stolen are so innumerable that we are unable to identify them all. However, one thing is clear: the car was not stolen due to Stephen's personal Karma.

The Real Meaning of Karma

What then is personal Karma? Karma means "action." This action takes three forms or Three Actions: 1) intentional thoughts, 2) speech, and 3) bodily action. In other words, Karma refers to what a person does, says and thinks, primarily in the religious context of cultivating oneself.[77] Actually, Karma is very optimistic, because it encourages us to cultivate ourselves

---

[77]. This does not mean that there is a religious realm separate from the everyday realm but rather points to the importance of one's motivation and the manner in which the actions are carried out. Karma needs to be framed within one's attempt to polish that gem within for spiritual Awakening and to improve oneself by behaving ethically.

religiously and morally to be the best we can be. This clearly differs from the notion of fate, which is typically pessimistic.

Second, Karma is applied primarily to *oneself* (first person). It should not be a means of judging others (third person), especially to explain why *other* people find themselves in unfortunate situations. So, we should not be saying to Stephen, "Oh, too bad, but that was your Karma," implying that he was fated or that he was being punished. Karma should not be the tool for *judging others*.

Unfortunately, in the long history of Buddhism, Karma was used to explain the reasons for the plight of others. For example, society's outcasts, the poor, and even the disabled were told to accept and resign themselves to their condition because they were told they were suffering due to their past actions, including in previous lives.

We have so far talked mostly about what personal Karma is *not*, so let us now discuss in greater deal what personal Karma *is*. As previously said, Karma refers to what a person does, says and thinks, primarily in the religious context of cultivating oneself toward the realization of Awakening.

When applied to Stephen's case, had he been cultivating himself he would have been better able to cope with the loss of his car. Instead, he was extremely upset, felt victimized and even blamed others, including the priest even though the priest had explained to Stephen that blessings do not play any part in the main purpose of Buddhism.

If Stephen had been studying the teachings to cultivate his thoughts, speech and bodily actions, he would have responded to the stolen car without being as upset and blaming others, and he might even have felt grateful that the situation wasn't worse. He was not physically hurt, which was a real possibility had he been around the car during the burglary. So, with a spiritually mature personal Karma, Stephen would have shown greater calm, understanding and even gratitude.

If you like, imagine a diagram that looks like a cross, with a *horizontal* axis and a *vertical* axis. The horizontal axis represents the objective conditions in which we live, our daily lives of family, school, work and society. This axis is wavy to represent the bumpy nature of our existence. Many people have *only* this axis or dimension, which makes them very vulnerable to the ups and downs of their bumpy lives.

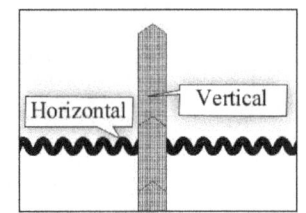

But those who cultivate their personal Karma possess a firm and stable *vertical* axis. They are better able to deal effectively with the ups and downs on their horizontal axis or their objective conditions. For example, if he had had a firm vertical axis, Stephen would not have become so upset, and he wouldn't have felt victimized or blamed others. He would naturally have been unhappy for having lost his car, but his anger would not have been so intense and lasted so long, and it wouldn't have impacted the rest of his daily life so negatively. In other words, his inner gem would have shined brighter.

The Eightfold Noble Path

The question now is to ask what are the ways for cultivating good Karma, thus enabling the jewel within to shine brighter. In Buddhism, there are a number of ways, but the most well-known is the Eightfold Noble Path. What are the eight that make up the Eightfold Noble Path? They are Right View, Right Intention, Right Speech, Right Conduct, Right Livelihood, Right Effort, Right Mindfulness and Right Concentration.

They can be seen as representing each of the eight spokes of the Wheel of Dharma, one of the main symbols of Buddhism. Also, these eight parts of the Path should not be seen as stages, where each one is completed before moving on to the next. Instead, all eight are practiced together as a set, as they complement and support each other.

Also, the Noble Path is not so much a set of commandments as it is a set of self-imposed guidelines for those seeking to experience greater meaning and fulfillment in life. It is voluntary and not something commanded by some external force from above or by a religious institution.

Further, each of the eight is referred to as "right," but they are not meant to be "right" as opposed to "wrong" in the *moral sense*. Instead, "right" is meant in the sense of being "appropriate" in keeping with truth, which then helps a person to lessen suffering and experience greater happiness.

In this sense, these are not *absolute* rules to be applied in *all* cases, *all* the time. At times we are unable to live up *fully* to the ideals of the Noble Path. This is true for those of us who are not living in a pristine and pure environment like the monks and nuns. So, I recommend that we apply these ideals in the spirit of "I shall try my best to carry them out" because life situations are not always black and white, and we do fail often.

1) Right View

Right View refers to our *understanding* of the Four Noble Truths and other Buddhist principles such as the Four Marks of Life.[78] Since we have already discussed the Four Noble Truths, you are requested to refer to the earlier discussions for details. (See Chapter 6)

As for the Four Marks of Life, they can be expressed in more "everyday" terms as: 1) "Life is a bumpy road;" 2) "Life is interdependent;" 3) "Life is impermanent;" and 4) "Life can be great." For greater details, you are asked to refer to the next chapter, which is devoted to the Four Marks of Life. (See Chapter 8)

2) Right Intention

Right Intention points to the *promise* we make to conduct our lives based on Right View. Right View was our understanding, but Right Intention is our firm promise to put our understanding into practice in our everyday lives.

Right View is the theory and Right Intention is our promise to put that theory into practice. In any sport, we learn the basic rules of the game (= theory) from the coach, but as we play the game we must have the strong intention to follow the rules (= promise).

3) Right Speech

Right Speech encourages us to refrain from four things: false speech; divisive speech; hurtful words; and idle talk.

False speech or lying is not allowed in almost all religions. So it requires no detailed explanation. It is simply the act of saying something that is different from the facts or opposite of what is in your heart.

Divisive speech includes slandering, backbiting and talk that can lead to hatred and disunity among individuals or groups of people.

Hurtful words include harsh, rude, hateful and abusive language that is hurtful to others.

Idle talk refers to the act of talking about things that have very little value, such as gossip, which is based on hearsay and is often used just to pass the time or to build a false sense of camaraderie, feeling we are right while others are wrong.

Buddhism discourages wrong speech because it is often carried out with G.A.S. or greed, anger/hatred, and stupidity/ignorance. However, when we practice Right Speech, it helps to reduce our G.A.S., as well as encouraging us to speak more pleasantly, thoughtfully and compassionately.

---

78. The Four Marks of Life are traditionally not included here, but I have taken the liberty to do so since they provide an appropriate Right View on life for contemporary people, particularly one that youths can easily understand.

4) Right Conduct

Right Conduct encourages us to refrain from killing, stealing and sexual misconduct.

Killing is the act of taking life, which includes human life. In the history of Buddhism, this teaching discouraged lay Buddhists (who are not monks or nuns) to stay away from occupations that involve killing, such as making and selling of arms and weapons.

Buddhists also stayed away from work that involved killing land animals, birds, fish and other living creatures. However, that does not mean that all Buddhists are vegetarian, for even the Buddha ate meat when offered. That is true even today for Theravada monks and lay people in Southeast Asian countries.[79] When they do so, they express their deep gratitude for the lives sacrificed and do their best not to waste them.

Stealing is simply the act of taking what does not belong to you. This, too, is one of the widely held prohibitions found in virtually all religions.

Refraining from sexual misconduct for Buddhist monks and nuns meant that they could not take part in any form of sexual activity, since they have taken vows of celibacy. For lay people, a Buddhist understanding is that sex has the potential to cause great harm and suffering if misused, but, on the other hand, it can be a source of pleasure and fulfillment between two people in a loving and committed relationship.

And it is true that it becomes a little more difficult to define what constitutes "misconduct" for people in different cultures and over time. However, the best way for those of us living today to understand "misconduct" is to understand that it means any action that causes *harm*. So, for someone in a committed relationship (such as marriage), having an affair would cause a lot of pain to that person's partner. Further, acts of obvious sexual misconduct such as sexual harassment, rape and sex with a minor constitute not only criminal behaviour but also cause enormous pain and emotional damage to the victims forever.

5) Right Livelihood

For monks and nuns, Right Livelihood prohibits them from engaging in activities that are unbecoming of spiritual seekers. Lay Buddhists are discouraged from being in occupations that go against the basic Buddhist ethical values.

One such value is refraining from killing, as mentioned before. Such

---

79. When Buddhism entered China and the rest of East Asia, especially the monks and nuns adopted vegetarian practices. Today many lay Buddhists are not strict vegetarians.

being the case, traditionally there have been occupations that are considered unsuitable. They include occupations that involve trading in arms and lethal weapons, as well as in the killing of animals.[80] Other unsuitable occupations are those that involve slavery, prostitution, and illegal drugs.

It is clear from this that Buddhism discouraged professions that bring harm to others. This is in line with the Buddhist position of strongly opposing any kind of war and aggressive acts, as seen in Buddha's well-known words,

> Hatred is not overcome by hatred, but only by acts of non-hatred is hatred overcome. [*Dhammapada*]

6) Right Effort

Right Effort is the focused, energetic will to foster positive and wholesome states of mind. There are four ways of accomplishing this, as explained traditionally: 1) to prevent negative and unwholesome states of mind from arising; 2) to put an end to negative and unwholesome states of mind that have already arisen; 3) to cultivate conditions for positive and wholesome states of mind that have not yet arisen; and 4) to foster and bring to perfection the positive and wholesome states of mind that have already arisen.

7) Right Mindfulness

Mindfulness is one form of meditation. In our view, Right Mindfulness is the most useful and accessible practice for lay people living in today's society, which is why millions of North Americans have either practiced it or are practicing it today. North Americans are practicing mindfulness not only in a spiritual context but also to reduce stress, increase focus, enhance physical immunity, etc. And they are doing it in hospitals, prisons, schools, military facilities and workplaces. Some of the largest companies such as Google, Nike and Apple are offering their employees the opportunity to practice mindfulness at the workplace.

Mindfulness practice calls for four objects of awareness, which are: 1) the activities of the body; 2) sensations or feelings; 3) activities of the mind; and 4) "objects" of the mind such as ideas, thoughts, and conceptions.

Of the four, the mindfulness of the first object (the activities of the

---

80. While Buddhists are discouraged from going into these occupations, we realize that some people may not have that choice. So, we should not be too quick to judge other people's choices and circumstances. Plus, those who are not vegetarians are able to enjoy their meat precisely because there are people working in the slaughterhouses.

body) is easiest for beginners to understand and practice. So, here, we will concentrate on this and leave the explanation of the other three (sensations, activities of the mind and the objects of the mind) for another occasion.

Now, this mindfulness of the activities of the body can further be categorized into three types: 1) breathing; 2) bodily movements; and 3) elements that make our body.

Breathing. We will first explain the mindfulness of *breathing*. To start, if we are able to do so, we sit with legs crossed, sitting on the floor with our back straight, at a 90 degree angle or perpendicular to the floor. This posture resembles what you often see in the images of the Buddha sitting in meditation.

However, for those of us who are lay persons living in the contemporary world, I believe we should be allowed to sit in chairs if we so prefer or need to. While practicing this form of mindfulness, our hands are placed naturally and comfortably on our lap.

We can practice mindfulness whenever we have a little time, for example, just before a game or a test, before going to bed, or riding in a car as passenger, but...*not* while we are *driving*!

As for our eyes, we can keep them half-opened or gently closed. You should choose whichever is more comfortable. If our eyes are open, our gaze can be cast downward a bit, perhaps about 45 degrees. We then breathe naturally through our *nose*, not our mouth. Breathing should also be very natural and not forced.

As for our thoughts, some people incorrectly think, "we should *not* think of anything" or "we need to *empty* our minds." For beginners, it is impossible to stop our thoughts and feelings from arising. We will not be able to repress them. Instead, we are invited to notice thoughts and feelings and then simply let them go in order to go back to awareness of our breathing. In other words, *we pay full attention* to our breathing. This can be done in a number of ways.

One way is to silently say "in" when we breathe in, and "out" when we breathe out. Another method is to direct our attention to the spot under our nostrils to pay attention to the fact that it feels cool when we breathe in, and it is warm when we breathe out. Or we can pay attention to the slight rise and fall of our abdomen; as we breathe in, our abdomen rises, at which time we can say silently to ourselves, "rising;" and as we breathe out, our abdomen falls, at which time we can say "falling."

Especially in the beginning, our mind will wander; various feelings and thoughts will crop up, making it awfully difficult to concentrate on our breathing. Actually, we cannot *prevent* thoughts and feelings from arising, because the seeds have been planted as the result of our past actions, and these thoughts and feelings are the inevitable fruit of such seeds. So, our objective is *not* to prevent to them or to try to think of nothing.

What we must do is to allow those feelings and thoughts to arise and then let them go. Let them come and go, but don't cling to them and get entangled with them. As we let our thoughts come and go, we return to paying attention to our breathing, just as a spider eventually returns to the centre of its web. Breathing is the centre of the web.

Thich Nhat Hanh, a well-known Buddhist monk and teacher who passed away recently, said that many people hate their bodies, but breathing helps them to become more acquainted and familiar with their bodies.

He would talk of a meditation teacher who begins her practice session by telling her students, "Let us be aware of our bodies. Breathing in, I know I am standing here in my body. Breathing out, I smile to my body." She encourages us to make peace with our body.

You can do this for several minutes or for however long you wish. Many people have found that even a few minutes of mindfulness practice will leave them feeling a little more settled and physically refreshed.

Bodily movement. The second category of mindfulness of the body is on our bodily movement. This calls for us to pay full attention to our bodily activities, such as putting on our clothes, listening to others, and eating our meals. Let's take the example of listening to someone else talk. As we all know, listening with undivided attention is not an easy task. However, with mindfulness practice, we can be trained to listen more fully and deeply to others when they are talking.

The same goes for eating. Often, we are not even aware of what we are eating, for while eating we may be watching television, looking at our smartphone, or be too absorbed in a conversation. We are, thus, encouraged to be mindful and aware of the food that is on our plates. If we are not aware of what we are eating, then we certainly cannot be savouring the food; this very frequently leaves us feeling emotionally unsatisfied.

However, mindfulness helps to ease this unsatisfactory feeling, while leading you to experience greater contentment. This sense of satisfaction or fulfillment cannot be explained logically. We simply need to practice and experience it!

Elements that make our body. Thirdly, with regard to the mindfulness of the elements of our body, the Buddha taught that our body is comprised of the elements of earth, water, fire and wind.

First, we become mindful of the *earth* element in us, which refers to the matters that are solid. So, there are earth elements inside of us as well as outside of us. When we realize that we are comprised of the same elements as things outside of us, then we see that we are intimately related to the rest of the universe.

Next, we pay attention to the *water* element within us, which makes up over 75 percent of our body. When we do, we realize that we are, again, deeply connected to the water that is outside us, whether it's in the form of rain or water in the rivers and the oceans.

The same is true for the *heat* element that is within us. Heat is found in the various processes of our body that manifest in the warmth of our body. And this is intimately connected to the heat outside of us, which ultimately is based on the sun, which is some 93 million miles or 150 million kilometers away.

Fourth is the *wind* element. This exists as air within us and as wind outside of us, as previously discussed in connection with mindfulness of breathing.

So, in meditating on the four elements, we become more aware of the components that make up our body as well as our body's essential connection to the outside world. This form of meditation helps us to realize that we are, indeed, "*one* with the universe."

8) Right Concentration

The last or the eighth on the list of parts of the Eightfold Noble Path is Right Concentration; its original Sanskrit is *dhyana*, from which we get the Japanese word "Zen."

Concentration, however, involves a very advanced set of practices mostly for monks and nuns. It aims for higher spiritual states that go far beyond what most ordinary people can attain. So we shall forgo discussing the details of Concentration until there is another opportunity to do so. Instead, you are encouraged to practice Mindfulness as was previously discussed, for you will surely reap much benefit physically, mentally and spiritually.

The Eight Seen as Three Learnings
Tiger Woods as Example

As we conclude this section, I wish to make mention of another well-known teaching called the Three Learnings, which help to simplify the Eightfold Path, thus, making the latter easier to grasp and remember. The Three Learnings are: 1) conduct; 2) meditation; and 3) wisdom.

Each of these is a category containing the appropriate parts of the Eightfold Noble Path:

Wisdom	**Conduct**	**Meditation**
Right View	Right Speech	Right Effort
Right Intention	Right Conduct	Right Mindfulness
	Right Livelihood	Right Concentration

The Three Learnings make it easy for us to realize that we need to cultivate the three main dimensions of ourselves. They are how we understand our lives and the world (Wisdom), how we act (Conduct), and how we train our mind (Meditation).

Let's take the case of a world-famous athlete, Tiger Woods, who, as mentioned earlier, is a Buddhist. Yes, I know, his talents and accomplishments are extraordinary, and you may feel that he will not be a good example.

However, even he has to exercise the Three Learnings in order to be at the top of his game. For example, he constantly studies and works on his form, whether it be his drives, approaches or putts. Before any tournament he studies the peculiarities of the course. An understanding is essential, even for someone especially gifted as Tiger Woods. And this represents the *wisdom* dimension of the Three Learnings.

At the same time, I am sure that Tiger Woods requires a lifestyle that includes a healthy diet, ample sleeping time, and a satisfying relationship with other people. His relationships, for example, would suffer if he were to speak harshly to his family and lie to his business associates. He could not afford the disruptions and upheavals in his personal life that would inevitably result from such behaviour.

Actually, Tiger Woods did conduct himself very poorly in ways that led to the breakup of his marriage. He then underwent years of difficulties in his personal life and a long slump in his golf game before rebuilding his life to regain his championship status.

For this reason, I considered not citing Tiger here as a model. However, I felt that we humans do make mistakes and that one failure should not be the reason for condemning Tiger forever. This is especially true when efforts are made to sincerely correct one's mistake. And I believe he has done that. Tiger has pulled himself together to conduct himself as in the past, which I believe contributed to his amazing comeback victory at the 2019 Masters Tournament.

So, proper conduct is necessary for a person to be physically and emotionally supported by others to do well in one's work, and this applies to everyone, including famous people like Tiger Woods. Here we see the *conduct* dimension.

The ability for golfers to concentrate on their game is very important. We have become accustomed to seeing Tiger Woods gaze intently at the ball and the hole. As he does so, thousands in the gallery look on, with millions more doing the same on television. While millions of eyes are on him, Tiger's eyes are on the ball and nothing else. And his ability to focus on the game is truly impressive.

In a TV interview that I once saw, Tiger attributed his ability to concentrate partly to the values of his Thai mother, for whom Buddhist meditation was a vital part of her Thai heritage. In any event, the ability to focus and concentrate on one's work is essential for success, whether you are Tiger Woods or any person in any line of work. This corresponds to the *meditation* dimension.

So, we can see the importance of cultivating the Three Learnings expressed through the Eightfold Noble Path. By cultivating ourselves in this way, we can develop the wisdom and the confidence to deal with many of the difficulties we face. We won't end up feeling as insecure and upset as Stephen, whose car was stolen as mentioned at the beginning of this chapter!

8 The Four Marks of Life

Relationship of the Eightfold Noble Path

WE WOULD NOW LIKE TO EXPLORE the teaching of the Four Marks of Life. As the name implies, these "marks" or "seals" are the teachings that Buddhists considered best represent their religion when compared to other religions. The Four Marks are a separate set of teachings from the Four Noble Truths, even though parts of them do overlap.

Here in this book, I would like to treat the two sets of teachings as an *integral set*, not only because they overlap in some areas but also because this will help readers to gain a unified understanding of the basic Buddhist teachings.[81]

In so doing, I wish to regard the Four Marks of Life as an important segment of the Eightfold Noble Path, which we just discussed. How then do the Four Marks of Life relate to the Eightfold Noble Path? They fall under Right View.[82]

1. Right View = Four Marks of Life
2. Right Intention
3. Right Speech
4. Right Conduct
5. Right Livelihood
6. Right Effort
7. Right Mindfulness
8. Right Concentration

The aim of Buddhist teaching is to help us awaken to truth, and to do so, we need to *view* our experiences, our life and the world in the *right* or *appropriate* way, thus, Right View. And the Four Marks of Life show us the details of how to do that.

---

81. Traditionally the Four Noble Truths and the Four Marks were not presented as a unified teaching, but I am bringing them together here to make it easier for readers to understand the basic Buddhist way of thinking and living.

82. Traditionally, the primary object of Right View was the Four Noble Truths.

The Four Marks of Life as a Whole

What are the Four Marks of Life? We will provide the traditional statement followed by an everyday expression for easier understanding.

- All Conditioned Phenomena are Suffering. (traditional)
    Rephrased, "Life is a bumpy road." (everyday)
- All Conditioned Phenomena lack substantial entity.
    Rephrased, "Life is interdependent."
- All Conditioned Phenomena are impermanent.
    Rephrased, "Life is impermanent."
- Nirvana is peaceful and tranquil.
    Rephrased, "Life can be great."

In order for us to be able to remember the Four Marks of Life, we have come up with a catchy and light-hearted set of acronyms. Their everyday expressions are Life is a **B**umpy road, Life is **I**nterdependent, Life is **I**mpermanent and Life can be **G**reat. By taking the first letters of Bumpy, Interdependent, Impermanent and Great, we get "BIIG." So, to remember the four, please "Think BIIG!"

Now, the opposite of Thinking BIIG, or the instinctual way is to view life as follows: Life should be a **S**mooth Road as opposed to Life is a Bumpy Road, Life should be **M**ine as opposed to Life is Interdependent, Life should **A**lways be the Same as opposed to Life is Impermanent, and Life is **L**ousy as opposed to Life can be Great."

And if we take the first letter of Smooth, Mine, Always and Lousy, we get SMAL. So, to remember them, "Don't think SMAL!" And, put together, "Think BIIG and Don't think SMAL!"[83]

A Buddhist View	Human Instinctual View
Life is a **B**umpy Road	Life should be a **S**mooth Road
Life is **I**nterdependent	Life should be **M**ine
Life is **I**mpermanent	Life should **A**lways be the Same
Life can be **G**reat	Life is **L**ousy
Think BIIG!	**Don't think SMAL!**

---

83. I hesitated to use these sets of acronyms because they have appeared in my previous books, but since they have helped many readers to remember this teaching, I decided to use them here as well.

Knowing the Four Marks Can Make You Happier

If you find yourself Thinking SMAL, do try to Think BIIG! Doing so will reduce suffering and make you happier.

It's not *wrong* to Think SMAL at times, since it is our human instinctual way to do so. In this competitive world, especially when you are young, you must Think SMAL at times. For example, to go to college or to pursue a career of your choice you must assume "Life is a Smooth Road" and "Life is Mine." If you don't, it would be hard to make plans and muster up the energy to work toward those goals.

However, life doesn't always go your way, and you might find yourself disappointed and even angry at life and the world. And you may get so disillusioned as to conclude that Life is Lousy and to think that life is not worth living. Such thinking could even lead to the "unthinkable," suicide.

I debated whether to include the following episode of my encounter with a suicide but decided to share it since it makes an important point. And it just may discourage someone and prevent a suicide from taking place. If you feel that you would rather avoid reading it, please skip the rest of this section.

A few years ago, I was on a commuter train. As the train approached a station, it made a sudden stop, jerking us passengers around. It was not a normal stop. Soon some of the station staff came around to look under the very car that I was riding in. An eerie feeling filled the entire car, for the passengers knew that someone had jumped onto the tracks and that the person's body was underneath us.

We've all heard about these train suicides, but it is totally different when it affects you personally like this. Well, after sitting there in a hushed car for about 15 minutes, I happened to look out the window, and they had pulled the body to the side of the tracks and had covered it with a blue tarp. Only a pair of shoes showed from under the edge of the tarp, and they looked like those of a young woman.

My immediate thoughts were, "Why does a young woman with the rest of her life ahead of her have to take her own life? How tragic! How sad!" Then, as a parent of three children myself, I thought of her parents, whose shock and pain must be untold and unfathomable. Then, I thought, maybe she would not have gone as far if she had some sound teachings to help her deal with whatever difficulties she was dealing with.

Buddhism Is a Voluntary Religion

So, it is with this kind of concern that I encourage all young people to have a sound and solid view of life, based on religion, philosophy or literature. Here, I am proposing Buddhism for you to consider, because it can provide you with that core outlook for dealing with the ups and downs of life.

Buddhism is a *voluntary* religion. You are not obligated to follow it. The Buddha claimed, "ehi passiko," meaning "come here and see [if you are interested]." You have a choice, and Buddhism does not force or command you to follow the teachings.

For example, when a teaching is presented it tells you there is a cause and effect relationship between your actions and the consequences of your actions. It is up to you to look at the consequence of your actions and to determine which action to take each subsequent moment. The decision is up to you.

This attitude applies to the Four Marks of Life. You are free to Think BIIG or Think SMAL. Whichever you choose, it will have its consequence and will make a difference in your life. Buddhism does not *force* you to choose one over the other, for, again, the decision is up to you.

We all have the capacity to exercise the power to make the right decision to achieve greater happiness for oneself and for others. We owe it to ourselves, to our loved ones, and to our world. If you are happy, you will have a positive impact on your family, friends and even strangers that you meet!

Applying the Teachings to Our Lives through a Wonderful Story

Speaking of applying them to our lives, let's see how "Thinking BIIG and not thinking SMAL" can assist us in dealing with the difficulties in our lives. To make a point, we'd like to refer to the four characters from the best-selling book *Who Moved My Cheese?* by Dr. Spencer Johnson.[84]

In a faraway land, there lived two mice named "Sniff" and "Scurry" and two little people named "Hem" and "Haw," who were as small as mice but looked and acted a lot like people today. Each day they ran through a maze looking for cheese to nourish them and make them happy. One day, the four

---

84. Spencer Johnson, *Who Moved My Cheese?* (G.P. Putnam's Sons, Inc., 1998). The book is now over 20 years old, but I have cited it here since I believe that younger readers today will still find it meaningful because the message is true in any age.

found a huge cheese near Cheese Station C. They were naturally overjoyed! They made themselves at home at Cheese Station C, and their life was going very well as they had plenty to eat every day. However, one day the cheese had disappeared completely!

Well, the two groups responded to the disappearance in stark contrast to each other. The mice Sniff and Scurry responded in keeping with "BIIG," while the little people Hem and Haw in accord with "SMAL."

The mice Sniff and Scurry were not surprised that the cheese had disappeared, for they had noticed that it had been getting smaller every day. If you constantly consume something, eventually it will be gone. Life is Impermanent! The cheese, too, does not last forever. Things change. And that change is often not what you wish or want. Life doesn't always go your way, and Sniff and Scurry fully understood life to be a Bumpy road!

Hem and Haw Thinking SMAL

On the other hand, when Hem and Haw found their cheese gone, they were completely unprepared. They screamed and yelled, "What! No cheese? It's not fair." For them, it was not the way things are supposed to be. They expected life to always go their way, reflecting the non-Buddhist outlook, "Life ought to be Smooth."

Further, the two little people were deeply upset because they felt that the cheese was theirs. They felt that they were entitled to the cheese and began to blame others for its disappearance. They yelled, "Who moved our cheese?" Hem, in particular, felt that way and insisted that the cheese was his and yelled, "The cheese was Mine."

To the contrary, the mice made no such claims. They knew that the cheese, which they had been enjoying, was the result of numerous interdependent causes and conditions that made it possible for the four of them to enjoy. And its disappearance, too, was due to the same principle of causes and conditions. The appearance and the disappearance of the cheese were due to causes far greater than any one mouse or little person could control. So, the mice knew better than to claim the cheese as their basic right or "Mine!"

When the cheese disappeared, Hem and Haw were caught totally off guard, for they had not been paying attention to the small changes taking place each day. They were too absorbed in their own delight and took for granted that the cheese would *Always* be there. They didn't want to face the truth that everything changes.

On the other hand, the mice Sniff and Scurry weren't surprised, since they were prepared for the change and wasted no time in looking for new cheese. Their actions corresponded with the outlook that "Life is *Impermanent.*"

For Hem and Haw, on the other hand, the disappearance of the cheese brought them misery. They refused to accept the situation, and, instead, clung to the way things were. As they waited for the cheese to return, they became mentally and physically exhausted and felt miserable and desperate. Their situation was simply *Lousy*!

Haw Thinking BIIG

To his credit, Haw began to reconsider their miserable situation and encouraged Hem to go with him to look for new cheese. However, the stubborn Hem refused. So Haw went forth by himself.

As he moved forward in the maze, Haw felt two kinds of anxiety. One was the anxiety of *leaving* their Station C, which had become home. The other was the anxiety of moving out into the *unknown*. We have all experienced this kind of situation, haven't we? For example, perhaps you remember feeling sad leaving elementary or middle school and, at the same time, feeling the anxiety of moving up to middle or high school.

As Haw moved out into the maze in search of the new cheese, his anxiety waned as he felt the *excitement* of going forward to see new things and the anticipation of new cheese. With his newly found joy and energy, he felt how foolish he was to have insisted on remaining at Station C even after the cheese had disappeared.

Now Haw realized that of the two kinds of anxieties (of leaving the familiar and venturing out into the unfamiliar), he would definitely take the *latter*. He scolded himself for not realizing that quicker.

Well, the mice had known that all along and had immediately set out in search of new cheese. It took them some time, but they did come upon a great supply of new cheese. They squealed with delight when they found what they were looking for, and it was the biggest store of cheese they had ever seen! So, for Sniff and Scurry, their situation was, indeed, *Great*.

As for Haw, he finally did arrive at the same cheese to his great delight. Haw saw that his mice friends had been there for some time from their big, popped bellies and happy smiles as they welcomed him. Haw regretted that Hem was still back there at Station C feeling miserable and *Lousy*.

The question for all of us is, "Which is the better way to go if we want to be happy and be at peace with ourselves, thinking SMAL like Hem and Haw (before he changed), or thinking BIIG like the mice Sniff and Scurry?" Well, the answer is quite obvious, but the decision is up to you.[85]

---

[85]. It is important to keep in mind that we humans tend to THINK SMAL precisely because to THINK SMAL is instinctual in nature, and it fosters self-preservation and self-promotion. However, that choice often leads to unhappiness.

10 Popular Passages, Metaphors, and Stories[86]

READERS ARE ENCOURAGED to become familiar with these popular sayings from the Buddha and the sages of the Buddhism. These 1) passages, 2) metaphors, and 3) stories are sure to benefit you, especially in times of doubt, anxiety, and disappointment.

Passages

Self-Reliance

> Make yourself the lamp.
> Make the teachings the lamp. *(Nibbana Sutta)*

Author's Comment: These are some of the final words that the Buddha left for his disciples before he passed on. The Buddha taught each of us to believe in ourselves (*Make yourself the lamp*) based on the truth (*Make the teachings the lamp*). The Buddha trusted our capacity to understand the truth *directly* and *personally*; he encouraged us not to simply believe that what someone else says is true. His confidence in us to do so was due partly to the jewel within each of us.

A Greater Victory

> To conquer oneself is a greater victory than to conquer thousands in a battle. *(Dhammapada)*

Comment: We all know people who are always trying to control other people. Such people are not happy people. To become a truly happy person, we must work on ourselves mentally and spiritually. When we succeed, it's a victory worth far more than the false victory of controlling others. There is

---

86. While the comments are by the author, most of the entries and their translation in this chapter are adopted from *Learning the Wisdom of Enlightenment* (BDK America, 2019), pp. 1–47.

no true happiness in controlling others against their will. Instead, knowing oneself and controlling oneself is the key to true happiness.

Value This Moment

> Do not regret what happened in the past.
> Do not long for what has yet to come in the future.
> By not suffering,
> By fully planting oneself in the present,
> You will be healthy in mind and body. *(Majjhima Nikaya)*

Comment: It's true that we are a product of the past and that we must prepare for the future. Many of you are studying or in training in order to realize the dreams you have for the future. However, at each moment we *live* only in the *here* and *now*! The Buddhist teachings help us to live *fully* in the here and now. We have already seen the modern American version of this passage, which concludes with a clever pun: "Yesterday is history, and tomorrow is a mystery. But this moment is a gift, and that is why we call it the *present*!"

The Mistakes of Others

> It is easy to point out the mistakes of others, but hard to admit one's own mistakes. *(Dhammapada)*

Comment: How true this is! However, it is difficult to put into practice, because we don't want to "look bad" in front of other people. However, if we want to grow as human beings and improve our relationships with family and friends, we must be willing to admit our mistakes and failings. No one is perfect, and we all make mistakes. To admit one's own mistake is not a sign of weakness but of *strength*. It's a sign of one's character and a prerequisite if you want your inner jewel to shine forth and if you wish to realize Awakening.

Overcoming Hatred

> Hatred is not overcome by hatred. Only by abandoning hatred, can hatred be overcome. This is an eternal truth. *(Dhammapada)*

Comment: This passage changed the course of history at the 1951 Peace Treaty of San Francisco, where 49 nations met to officially conclude the war with Japan. Many nations wanted to punish Japan and extract enormous compensation from Japan for the damages it had caused during the war. In contrast, Junius Richard Jayewardene, representing Ceylon (now Sri Lanka), cited this passage, "Hatred ceases not by hatred but by love," which was well received and helped to sway the delegates to minimize the compensation sought from Japan. With minimal economic burden, Japan went on to become a peaceful and thriving nation after World War II, hosting two Olympic games.

In contrast, I believe that the feelings of revenge and hate in reaction to the 9/11 terrorist attack became one of the driving forces for the American invasion of Iraq in 2003. This has caused untold suffering for the Iraqi people and contributed to the instability of the region and the rise of the Islamic State. And over 6,000 American soldiers died during this conflict that lasted about ten years.

Canada, despite not joining the invading coalition, still participated in the conflict in Iraq, joining a number of non-belligerent nations in helping to rebuild the country post-invasion, including the training of Iraqi police and army officers, and contributing approximately $300 million towards this effort.

A Flower Without Fragrance

> To utter pleasant words without practicing them is like a radiant flower without fragrance. *(Dhammapada)*

Comment: This passage is warning us against being "all talk and no action." You probably know such people. If you do, you probably do not want to be around them. Why? It's because they are not trustworthy. They probably do not fully believe what they say, because if they did, their actions would match their words. As discussed earlier, the Three Actions of speech, body and mind should be in sync with each other. (See p. 88)

Preciousness

> Difficult it is to be born a human.
> Grateful I am for the life that I now have.
> Difficult it is for the Buddha to appear in the world.
> Grateful I am for being able to listen to the Buddha's teachings.
> *(Dhammapada)*

Comment: How rare it is to be born a human! The metaphor of the Turtle and the Floating Piece of Wood in a Buddhist story conveys this truth. On the surface of an immense ocean floats a piece of wood. In it there is a hole a few inches in diameter. A sea turtle that lives at the bottom of the ocean comes up to the surface once every hundred years. The chance of that turtle coming up to the surface and popping its head right into the hole in the wood that's floating in an immensely vast ocean is the same as that of being born a human being!

So, let us not waste our human life, and let us realize our dreams for our lives and be of service to others. According to Buddhism, the most important goal in life is to realize Awakening, which is made possible by the Buddha's teachings. That is why we also celebrate the fact that the Buddha appeared in the world to show us the way!

Essence of the Teachings

> To avoid all evil, to seek the good, to keep the mind pure: this is the essence of Buddha's teaching. *(Dhammapada)*

Comment: The first part of this passage, "to avoid all evil, to seek the good," is common to many other religions. However, it's the *last* phrase, "to keep the mind pure" that Buddhism stresses probably more than many other religions. That is because the first part of the sentence ("to avoid all evil, to seek the good") is a *means* to realize the pure mind, which is the aim of Buddhism. The aim in Buddhism is not only to be good in a moral and ethical sense but also to make *our mind pure*, which means that our G.A.S. (greed, anger/hatred and stupidity) decreases. When we make our mind pure, we become happier and more at peace within. And that pure mind can be achieved by *seeing life correctly* as expressed through the Four Marks of Existence and realized by cultivating the Eightfold Noble Path.

Metaphors

The Two-Headed Bird

> There once lived a bird with two heads. The rear head resented the front head, which was able to eat far more because it was in the front of the body. As the rear head's irritation turned to strong jealousy and then to hatred of the front head, the rear head wanted to hurt the front head by secretly slipping a poison

into the food the front head was eating.[87] Well, the front head ate the poison and became really sick. However, the rear head soon also became sick! On account of its jealousy and hatred, the rear head had forgotten that it and the front head shared the same body! *(Samyukta-ratna-pitaka sutra)*

Comment: As the second of the Four Marks of Life states, we are interconnected and interdependent. This truth is manifested in the nature of our globalized economy and the solutions to climate change. Like the rear head of the bird, if we *punish* other countries too harshly with high tariffs, then they retaliate by not buying our products. So, we all lose.

On the other hand, the front head should have been more sensitive to how the rear head was feeling. If it were, it would have noticed that the rear head was not happy because of the fact that it was not getting the same amount of food. The front head could have prevented the rear head's spiteful action.

Also, young readers of this book should be especially concerned about global climate change, because your generation will be the one more impacted. What another country on the other side of the earth fails to do can have devastating consequences for us, and the same is true for what our country fails to do for the rest of the world.

The Poisoned Arrow

Suppose a poisoned arrow pierced a man, and his relatives and friends got together to call a surgeon to have the arrow removed and the wound treated. But what if the wounded man objects, saying, "Wait a minute. Before you pull it out, I want to know who shot this arrow. Was it a man or a woman? Was it someone of noble birth or was it a peasant? What was the bow made of? Was it a big bow or a small bow that shot the arrow? Was it made of wood or bamboo? What was the bowstring made of? Was it made of fiber or of gut? Was the arrow made of rattan or of reed? What feathers were used? Before you extract the arrow, I want to know all about these things."

Before all this information can be secured, no doubt, the

---

87 In the traditional way of telling this metaphor, the rear head itself eats the poison, which makes the point harder to understand. So, I have "rearranged" it to make more sense by having the rear head poison the front head.

poison will have had time to circulate through his body and the man may die. The first duty is to remove the arrow, and prevent its poison from spreading. *(Majjhima Nikaya)*

Comment: The arrow represents suffering. If he wants to live and be happy, the man should pull out the arrow rather than waste time by asking all these intellectual questions. These questions not only do not help his predicament but delay pulling out the arrow, putting his life in grave danger.

Buddhism is a "first-person" religion, which means that I need to acknowledge the fact that "*I* am shot" and then *I* need to concentrate on pulling that arrow out. Some of you may feel that you are not yet shot. If that is the case, more power to you.

However, in the long course of life, you will certainly be pierced by at least one arrow. Before this happens, it might help you to understand what Buddhism has to say, for you will be better prepared to pull out the poison arrow of suffering.

And if you feel that you have been shot, like many of us do, let us then concentrate on pulling that arrow out. This means to learn and practice the teachings earnestly as *your own* urgent, existential problem. You should not be stuck asking useless questions, which are merely intellectual in nature.

Three Kinds of Letters

> There are three kinds of people in the world. The first are those who are like letters carved in rock; they easily give way to anger and retain their angry thoughts for a long time. The second are those who are like letters written in sand; they give way to anger also, but their angry thoughts quickly pass away. The third are those who are like letters written on running water; they do not retain their passing thoughts; they let abuse and uncomfortable gossip pass by unnoticed; and their minds are always pure and undisturbed. *(Anguttara Nikaya)*

Comment: This metaphor has to do with how we respond to anger. People whose mentality is like the letters carved in *rock* get extremely angry and hold on to their anger for a long time. Often, they just can't shake off their anger. Their anger negatively affects the rest of their daily activities so that they are not able to concentrate on their studies or work and cannot sleep well. And the second group is comprised of people who are like the letters drawn in the *sand*. They are like most people, who get upset or angry and feel bad for some period of time.

However, wouldn't we all want to be like those of the last group? They are like letters written on *running water*. It does not mean that they are indifferent or do not care about others and the world. They remain confident in themselves and caring of others but do not allow abuses, gossip and unpleasant things to affect them negatively.

If they get angry, it is because they want to help *other* people who are suffering from injustices or being treated unfairly. Like Gandhi, Martin Luther King and the Dalai Lama, they feel "justified" anger. However, their minds, at their core, are like the pure, running water.

Lotus Flowers Emerging from the Mud

> Just as pure and fragrant lotus flowers grow out of the mud of a swamp rather than out of the clean loam of an upland field, so from the muck of worldly passions springs the pure Enlightenment of Buddhahood. Even the mistaken views of heretics and the delusions of worldly passions may be the seeds for Buddhahood.
>
> Enlightenment is a precious pearl. A person must descend to the bottom of the sea, braving all dangers of jagged coral and vicious sharks. That person must face the perils of worldly passion in order to secure the precious pearl of Enlightenment. One must first be lost among the mountainous crags of egoism and selfishness before there will be an awakening of the desire to find a path that will lead that person to Enlightenment.
> (*Vimalakirti-nirdesha Sutra*)

Comment: When we recall our greatest joys in life, they were often preceded by hardships, disappointments or hard work. So, out of the *mud* grew the *lotus flower*! The mud symbolizes two things, shortcomings and unhappiness. Because of our shortcomings, we try hard not to make the same mistakes and aspire to do better. And because of our unhappiness, we strive to find ways to become happier. And when we achieve our aims, we come to realize the lotus flower of improvement and happiness!

I am sure many of you have experienced a disappointing loss on a sports team, but it was followed by a comeback in the next season to gain a redeeming win. This was made possible on account of the entire team's members rallying together to work hard to correct the shortcomings and to improve the team's performance.

Regarding the second point, that of happiness, it was the heart-breaking separation from my first girlfriend that motivated me to learn from my mistakes. That effort contributed to making my subsequent relationship with my wife of 43 years become the treasure or the lotus flower of my life.

So, in Buddhism shortcomings and improvements as well as unhappiness and happiness are seen as one, just as the lotus flower grows out of the mud! This means that we too need to face up to the "negatives" in life, which serve as the catalyst and motivation to realize the "positives" in life.

Parable of an Old Well

> Here is another allegory. A man who committed a crime is running away. Some guards are following him, so he tries to hide by descending into a well by means of some vines growing down the sides. As he descends he sees vipers (poisonous snakes) at the bottom of the well, so he decides to cling to the vine for safety. After a while his arms get tired, and he notices two mice, one white and the other black, gnawing at the vine.
>
> If the vine breaks, he will fall to the vipers and perish. Suddenly, on looking upward, he notices just above his face a beehive from which occasionally falls a drop of honey. The man, forgetting all his danger, tastes the honey with delight.
>
> "A man" means one who is born to suffer and die alone. "Guards" and "vipers" refer to the body with all its desires. "Vines" refer to the continuity of human life. "Two mice, one white and the other black" indicate fleeting time, days and nights, and the passing years. "Honey" indicates the physical pleasures that lure suffering beings into distractions as the years pass by.
>
> *(Sutra of the Parables)*

Comment: At first sight, I am sure that this parable might strike some readers as frightening. But please note that this is how life would be if you are *without* any spiritual or ethical guidance.[88] For us, we can avoid being in this frightening predicament if we follow the Buddhist teachings.

Please note that in Buddhism, there is no Satan or devil that tempts us, or God who judges our faithfulness to him. The cause of suffering lies in our Karmic action, how we think, speak and act in our daily lives. Of course, as discussed earlier, all of us experience difficulties, but it is the quality of

---

88 I believe that a person can be spiritual and ethical without being religious or belonging to a religious organization.

our minds that determines how well we face up to difficulties in a positive way, or how much we suffer. And we have the capacity to determine that by letting our jewel within shine forth; this means to let our minds see truth and to live according to the truth.

Stories

Losing a Child and Mustard Seeds

Once there was a young woman named Kisagotami, the wife of a wealthy man, who lost her mind because of the death of her child. She took the dead child in her arms and went from house to house begging people to heal the child.

Of course, they could do nothing for her, but finally a follower of Buddha advised her to see the Blessed One, who was then staying at Jetavana, and so she carried the dead child to Buddha.

The Blessed One looked at her with sympathy and said: "To heal the child I need some mustard seeds; go and beg for four or five mustard seeds from some home where death has never entered."

Filled with hope, the distraught woman went out to look for a house where death had never entered, but her efforts were in vain. At last, she was obliged to return to Buddha. In his quiet presence, her mind cleared and she understood the meaning of his words. She took the child's body away and buried it, and then returned to Buddha and became one of his disciples.

(*Therigatha Atthakatha*, or *Commentary on the Poems by Nuns*)

Comment: Actually, every house she visited had mustard seeds, used as spices in the kitchen, but no house could satisfy the other condition: "a home where death has never entered." Initially the grieving mother was confident about finding such a home. However, when she could not find any such a home, she came to realize that she was not *alone* in losing a loved one and that death affects every home. In other words, death is universal.

Most of us know this in our heads but do not really *live* it. Instead, we think that we have all the time in the world. So, we end up wasting time on frivolous activities.

Steve Jobs, who seriously practiced Buddhist meditation as a young adult, encouraged college graduates that the awareness of his eventual death made a huge difference in his life. It helped him to make bold decisions and not to be overly concerned by what other people thought of him or his decisions. Such awareness about death does not make us sad and gloomy but instead helps us become more alert and appreciative of life, encouraging us to live more fully and deeply.

A Third Storey Without a Foundation

Once there was a wealthy but foolish man. When he saw a beautiful three-storey house owned by another man, he envied it and made up his mind to have one built just like it, thinking he was himself just as wealthy. He called in a carpenter and ordered the carpenter to build it. The carpenter consented and immediately began to construct the foundation, the first storey, the second storey, and then the third storey. The wealthy man noticed this with irritation and said, "I don't want a foundation or a first storey or a second storey. I just want the beautiful third storey. Build it quickly."

A foolish man always thinks only of the results, and is impatient about putting in the effort that is necessary to get good results. No good can be attained without proper effort, just as there can be no third storey without the foundation and the first and second storeys. *(Upama-shakata-sutra)*

Comment: The point of the story is quite obvious, so I shall make no further comment except to encourage all of us to build a strong foundation by working on the fundamentals of whatever we aspire to do in life.

Harp Strings

There was a young man named Srona who was born into a wealthy family but was of delicate health. He was very earnest about gaining Enlightenment and became a disciple of the Blessed One. On the path to Enlightenment, he tried so hard that finally his feet bled.

The Blessed One pitied him and said, "Srona, my boy, did you ever study the harp at your home? You know that a harp does not make music if the strings are stretched too tightly or too loosely. It makes music only when the strings are stretched just right.

"The training for Enlightenment is just like adjusting the harp strings. You cannot attain Enlightenment if you stretch the strings of your mind too loosely or too tightly. You must be considerate and act wisely."

Srona found these words very helpful and finally gained what he sought. *(Mahavagga)*

Comment: This story points out the flaws of going to the *extreme* when trying to achieve one's aim in life, including that of Awakening or Enlightenment. If you recall, Siddhartha attained Awakening as the result of avoiding the extremes, a life of pleasure on one hand and a life of austere practices on the other. (See p. 45) His austere practices allowed him to have only one drop of water and one grain of rice a day, reducing him to skin and bones and leaving him without any energy to carry out the practices. Srona committed the same mistake by subjecting himself to extreme rigour, ending up being like the harp strings that are too tightly stretched.

Offering of Garments

When Syamavati, the queen-consort of King Udayana, offered Ananda 500 garments, Ananda received them with great satisfaction.

The King, hearing of it, suspected Ananda of dishonesty, so he went to Ananda and asked what he was going to do with these 500 robes.

Ananda replied: "Oh King, many of the monks are in rags, so I am going to distribute the garments among the brothers."

"What will you do with the old garments?"

"We will make bed covers out of them."

"What will you do with the old bed covers when they wear out?"

"We will make pillowcases."

"What will you do with the old pillowcases?"

"We will make floor coverings out of them."

"What will you do with the old floor coverings?"

"We will use them for foot towels."

"What will you do with the old foot towels?"

"We will use them as floor mops."

"What will you do with the old mops?"

"Your Highness, we will tear them into pieces, mix them with mud and use the mud to plaster house walls."

Every article entrusted to us must be used with good care in some useful way, because it is not "ours" but is only entrusted to us temporarily. *(Samyukta-ratna-pitaka-sutra)*

Comment: We definitely need more of Ananda's spirit of conservation! I feel that we waste so much in our throwaway culture. We throw away everything from used plastic cups and utensils to all kinds of electronic gadgets. The ocean is now cluttered with millions of tons of debris, especially plastic. All of this waste is happening in the name of convenience and made possible by cheaply available raw resources including those extracted from the earth, and manufactured by people who are poorly paid. So, we really need to adopt Ananda's way of treating material things with care, reverence and without wasting.

Gratitude to a Bamboo Thicket

In a bamboo thicket at the foot of the Himalayan Mountains, there once lived a parrot together with many other animals and birds. One day a fire started in the thicket from the friction of the bamboo stalks rubbing against each other in a strong wind, and the birds and animals were frightened and confused. The parrot, feeling compassion for their fear and suffering, and wishing to repay the kindness he had received in the bamboo thicket where he was allowed to shelter himself, tried to do all he could to save the other creatures. He dipped himself in a pond nearby and flew over the fire and shook off the drops of water to extinguish the fire. He repeated this diligently with a heart of compassion out of gratitude to the bamboo thicket.

This spirit of kindness and self-sacrifice was noticed by a heavenly god, who came down from the sky and said to the parrot, "You have a gallant mind, but what good do you expect to accomplish with a few drops of water against this great fire?" The parrot answered, "There is nothing that cannot be accomplished by the spirit of gratitude and self-sacrifice. I will try over and over again and then over again in my next life." The great god was impressed by the parrot's spirit and together they extinguished the fire. *(Samyukta-ratna-pitaka-sutra)*

Comment: We cannot help but be moved by the parrot's determination and effort to put out the fire, even though it seems like a lost cause. We may feel the same way about how much each of us can contribute to tackling huge social problems, such as poverty, discrimination, and climate change. But the parrot teaches us an important lesson. That lesson is that if all of us did our *small* part, then we *collectively* will become a huge force to accomplish what appears to be an impossible task.

Part Three

In Daily Life

10 Issues and Problems in Daily Life

BEFORE OFFERING MY RESPONSE to each of the ten issues and problems, I wish to first mention five basic *principles* that apply to all of them.

1. Life is a Bumpy Road. As the Buddha taught, life is truly a bumpy road. It is not a smooth road. Things often don't go our way. That's a fact of life, which means everyone is in the same boat. So if things don't go your way, you are not being punished, and it is not necessarily your fault or due to fate.

2. No divine or supernatural being who punishes and tests. Buddhism does not believe in a divine or supernatural being somewhere "out there," who punishes or tests you. Things happen on account of a whole host of cause-and-effect relationships, which are mostly beyond your control. For example, you were late to school, but it was because the bus was late, which was beyond your control.

However, whether you suffer or not is up to you. We cannot always control *our situation*, but we can control *our attitude* or how we think about that situation. This way of thinking is expressed in the concept of the horizontal axis and the vertical axis. (See p. 89)

3. Turning problems to opportunities. We all have the ability to turn problems into opportunities to learn about life, the world, and about ourselves. And this helps to deepen our ethical and spiritual understanding to make us stronger and wiser in dealing with our future problems and challenges.

4. First person. Buddhism is a "first person" religion. This means that we should face up to the problems of life as a *personal* matter first and foremost. And the solutions must come to you in ways that are personal and unique to yourself, which is the only way that you can be truly satisfied and fulfilled. Further, you cannot help others well if you have not helped yourself first. This is like when in an airplane emergency situation, we are instructed to put on one's own air mask *first* before helping anyone else.

5. Importance of physical well-being. Buddhism, like other religions, emphasizes not only the mind (the mental and the spiritual) but also the *body* as well. Body and mind are not separate. How we feel and think is often influenced by how our body is doing. If you haven't slept all night, you can't think straight and will become grouchy and you're probably a miserable person to be around. This is why Buddhist practice calls for the Three Learnings, which consist of 1) conduct, 2) meditation and 3) wisdom, to be practiced as a set. For conduct and meditation, taking good care of our bodies is vital! Many people have disabilities and chronic illnesses, but a society that cares for all helps everyone to enjoy as much physical well-being as is possible.

The following ten situations represent some of the frequent problems and issues that many young people wrestle with. If they apply to you, I hope that my response will be of some benefit to you.

Losing a Match in Sports
A seventeen-year-old's story

> Our basketball team lost an important game in overtime by just two points. I'm so upset and disappointed, especially because it was a team that we had beaten last year. Plus, we really practiced hard and felt that we were well prepared for the game. I feel like God was not on our side this time.

I'm sorry to hear about the loss and that you are upset and really disappointed. Although it can be hard to understand, from a Buddhist perspective, there is no such God that can determine the outcomes of basketball games.

As previously discussed, we believe that things happen due to one of the two basic categories of cause and effect, the "objective conditions." (See pp. 106, 108) The objective conditions point to a myriad of circumstances that contributed to the outcome of the game. The outcome is due not to one or two causes that you can isolate. So, you should not blame yourselves, your coach or even the referees.

Next, it will be for your own benefit and well-being to find a way to overcome your disappointment and the frustration of losing. Do remember that Life is a Bumpy Road. It won't always go your way. So, losing is part of life. The famed National Basketball Association basketball coach Phil Jackson said that "losing is as integral a part of the dance as winning." So, to lose is not a failure or reason to be embarrassed. Coach Jackson further encouraged us: "Buddhism teaches us that by accepting death, you discover life. Similarly, only by acknowledging the possibility of defeat can you fully experience the joy of competition."[89]

What is important is to bounce back and to be ready for the next game. You should not and cannot be hung up on what happened in the past. You cannot change the past, but you can try to change the future. You can learn from mistakes in past games, so as not to repeat the same mistakes in the future. At the same time, do see what you can do to build on what your team did well the last time. So do turn this loss into a chance to do better the next time.

Strict Parents
A fifteen-year-old's story

> I think that my parents are too strict. It's clear when I see how my friends' parents are. For example, I have a 10 o'clock curfew, can't go on a date till I turn 17, and they force me to take piano lessons even though I don't have much time to practice. Plus, I have to help with the chores around the house, like taking out the garbage, doing yard work, and cleaning the bathroom once a week. None of my friends are doing chores. It's only me.

First of all, a Buddhist approach would be to understand the nature of your problem. When you do so, you might see that this problem is the fifth of the Eight Kinds of Suffering, which is "having to face people and situations we don't like."

Secondly, have you ever sat down and talked with your parents about how you feel about the way they are raising you? If you haven't, you are encouraged to do so, because the Buddhist approach is to "face up" to problems instead of avoiding them.

When we encounter a situation, we don't like, we have three basic options. They are: 1) to leave the situation; 2) to accept the situation as it is; and 3) try to improve the situation by working things out. The first is not a realistic option because you are a minor and still a member of the family. Plus, I doubt that you would want to *leave* the family that you love. If you choose the second option, you should accept how things are and no longer complain about your situation.

The third option is to face up to the problem and to work things out directly with the persons involved. By doing so, it's possible that you and your parents will have a better understanding of each other. You can ask them to explain the reasons for their rules, while you explain to them that

---

89 Phil Jackson, *Sacred Hoops: Spiritual Lessons of a Hardwood Warrior* (Hyperion, 1995), p. 202.

you feel that they are being much stricter than your friends' parents.

You probably can become more accepting if you hear their reasons. That's because you will come to understand that your parents have your welfare in mind when they set the rules. Hopefully for you, they ease up on the rules a bit in response to your wishes.

But even if they don't, you've *faced up* to your problem and tried to resolve it by trying to understand your parents and to work things out. You could also talk with a trusted friend, teacher or minister who will not only empathize with your predicament but also provide a fresh perspective on the issue.

In the end, I am confident that these honest discussions with your parents and trusted people can only but contribute to changes for the better!

Breaking Up
A twenty-one-year-old's story

> My boyfriend and I have been seeing each other for one year now, but he suddenly broke up with me without any warning. I am devastated. Even though we had some problems, we were trying to work things out. I wish he could have tried harder to make things better. I hear from my friends that he may have found someone else, which hurts me even more.

Yes, I hear you! When I was your age, I went through something very similar. So, you are not alone. It hurts, doesn't it? It wouldn't be right if it didn't, for this person means a lot to you. It hurts also because you feel rejected, and your ego has been bruised.

I know it is a cliché, but "time does heal." But in order to heal a bit quicker and to learn from this, let me share some ways of looking at it from a Buddhist perspective. Again, an important Buddhist perspective is to turn this difficulty into a learning experience toward greater understanding about life and for moving toward Awakening.

First of all, this type of suffering is the sixth among the Eight Kinds of Suffering that Buddha talked about, "separating from persons and situations we like." (See p. 79) This can take the form of separation through death but also, as in your case, separation while alive.

Secondly, the truth of impermanence may help you to accept the situation. (See pp. 127–128)* It points to the fact that all things, including relationships, will eventually end. If it's any consolation to you, many other relationships that begin during college end within a few years. The chance of such relationships culminating in marriage is even less. So, what happened to you is par for the course. That may not be a consolation, but such is the harsh reality!

Thirdly, the truth of interdependence, (See pp. 127–128)* shows us that your relationship with your boyfriend was the result of immeasurable causes and conditions that brought you together. For example, you lived in the same period in history and in the same location, both of which carry their sets of causes and conditions that stretch indefinitely back in time and space. Yes, you did take the initiative to make the relationship, but your effort was just a tiny drop in an ocean of factors that brought you together.

That means that when the causes and conditions *change* to bring about an end to the relationship, *any* effort by you will not be able to change the situation. So, no matter how hard you wish or try to save the relationship, it will be to no avail, for our relationships are the result of things that are often far beyond your control.

You may be feeling, "There is no one else better for me than he is. He was the *only* one for me. My life would be worthless without him." Well, it may be hard for you to see it now, but many people in your situation have gone on to find another person, who turned out to be even a better fit for them.

Finally, the fact that things did not work out between you two often means that there were some fundamental mismatches between you. You may not be able see that *now*. In my own case, it was only a number of years later after we broke up that I came to see and admit to basic incompatibility in our personalities. It became evident only in hindsight. So, in a way, it may be good that problems surfaced now, rather than later, after the two of you may have gotten married.

Death of a Family Member
An eighteen-year-old's story

> My 75-year-old grandfather passed away suddenly. The cause of death was pneumonia. We were all shocked because he was in pretty good health. He lived nearby so I saw him often. Grandpa was my favourite among all my four grandparents. He took me fishing and told me many stories about his life and his younger years. I feel angry that he was taken away from us; he should have lived for at least another 10 years.

This must be difficult for you, especially since he was in quite good health and was your favourite grandparent. Plus, these days, 75 is quite a young age to die. So, it's natural for you to feel regret and sadness. If you didn't feel them, it would be unnatural.

The Buddha acknowledged the kind of suffering you are going through, and he identified "death" as one of the Eight Kinds of Sufferings. (See p. 79) Also, what you are experiencing can be counted as the sixth suffering, "separating from persons and situations we like." This is the same category as the previous story of a romantic breakup, though in this situation it's your grandparent, and your separation from him is through death.

Amidst your pain of losing your grandfather, there are ways to lessen your sadness and to learn from the loss. First of all, what is important is not always the *length* of life but *how* one lived his or her life. From what you have told me about him, your grandfather lived a fulfilling life, having had meaningful and enjoyable work for over 40 years. He was blessed with a loving family, who took great care of him till the end. And you were an important part of that.

It would serve you well to remember all the good times you had with him, especially those fishing trips. Also, ask yourself what lessons you learned from him. If one of them is the importance of "perseverance," then when you find yourself persevering toward a goal, think of your grandpa and feel that he is with you in spirit. Then, you will find extra strength to try even harder and longer with his "presence" in your thoughts. So, he *continues* to live in you when you put into practice what he shared and taught you.

The passing of your grandfather also awakens you to the truth of impermanence, especially in our relationships with our loved ones. So, you should realize that your parents, brothers, sisters and friends will not be around *forever*, and no one knows when they will depart from your life. As the Buddha stated, the one truth about life after being born is that we will die.

You may find this kind of talk to be unnecessarily pessimistic, but it is a fact and a reality. If you recall, Buddhism calls on us to see reality as it *truly is*, not how *we want* to see it. Impermanence is reality. Actually, the reality of impermanence should not make you sad but, to the contrary, encourage you to *cherish* the loved ones in your life here and now and to actively *adjust* to the changes!

Envious of My Successful Friends
A twenty-five-year-old's story

I went into a field that doesn't pay that well. While I enjoy my job and find it meaningful, I can't help feeling a bit envious of my classmates and friends who are in much better paying jobs. Tom, my best friend from high school, is a software engineer, and he now owns a house, while I struggle just to pay my rent and have no idea when, if ever, I might be able to buy a house.

As the gems in Indra's Net of Jewels showed, each one of us is unique. There are no two gems that are exactly alike. So, the uniqueness of each jewel is to be affirmed. In the same way, you should appreciate and affirm what is unique about you. This means that you should not be comparing yourself with others. Of course, that's easier said than done.

One way to help you to not compare yourself with others is to take pride in the choices that *you* made about your profession. You say you find meaning in your line of work and enjoy your job. That is a huge accomplishment. I would like to congratulate you on having found such work, especially a job that serves to benefit those who are less fortunate than others or is nurturing the next generation.

Unfortunately, our society places too much premium on material things, but you should take pride in your work for the good that you do for the community. Please cherish that sense of meaning you have in your work, because from a Buddhist perspective that is far more important than what this excessively materialistic society considers important. Such expectations are superficial, but your pride in your work is deeper and will serve to provide true meaning and fulfillment in the long run.

Besides, at 25 years of age, you are still very young. Compared to me, you are far ahead of the game. Having spent 15 years in graduate school to earn my Ph.D. in Buddhist studies (including two Masters degrees), I did not have a full-time job till I was almost 40 years old. And my position as a junior faculty member at a Buddhist seminary and a minister at a temple were hardly good paying jobs! Nevertheless, we managed to live a modestly comfortable life and to raise three children.

So, with careful allocation of funds and a modest lifestyle, you should be able to have enough material things. After all, if you live a middle class lifestyle in Canada, you are wealthier than the majority of the people in the rest of the world. More importantly, the mental and spiritual well-being of your meaningful work will far outweigh what you may have gotten from a bigger house and a more extravagant material lifestyle.

Uneasy About Being a Buddhist
A thirteen-year-old's story

> I feel uneasy when people ask me about my religion because Buddhism is not that well-known and is a minor religion in this country. Plus, I am a Buddhist mostly because my parents are Buddhist. One of my Christian friends felt sad for me because she says that I will go to hell when I die. I know that that is not true, but it still doesn't make me feel better.

It sounds like your discomfort comes from the fact that you don't know much about Buddhism. But you can turn this into an opportunity to become better informed about your religion by learning more about it. When you do, you will gain greater understanding and confidence so that you would not be bothered by what others say about Buddhism. You will, for example, learn that, as discussed already, Buddhism is one the three major world religions and is the oldest among them. This means that like Christianity and Islam, Buddhism has followers in vast areas of the world. And, as we learned, in more recent years it has become more popular in Europe and North America, especially in this country.

There are now many people in Canada who are Buddhists or who are Nightstand Buddhists. (See p. 18) They include people whose names are well-known, for example the late singer, song writer and poet Leonard Cohen, a well-known hockey coach Jim Bedard, singer/songwriters Alanis Morissette and k.d. Lang, and actor Jim Carey, as well as many more who are only well-known in their own communities.

Plus, Buddhism has been a relatively peaceful religion. You will not see Buddhists engaged in large scale fighting over differences in the teachings or using force to convert others to Buddhism. Of course, as in any large religious group, there have been so-called Buddhists who have fanned the flames of hatred and violence. I find this deeply regrettable and sad, but such Buddhists are a tiny, tiny minority.

Again, please do learn more about the teachings and practice them in your daily life. *That* will assure greater confidence in Buddhism as *your* religion of personal choice!

Bullying and Prejudice
A fourteen-year-old's story

> I feel bad that some of my classmates pick on some of the kids in our class. I think they do that because the bullied kids are immigrants and don't speak English well. I've also heard these bullying classmates make some nasty racial comments.

You are right to feel bad, for there should be no place in our society for bullying to take place. Unfortunately, however, it does take place even though many people try to prevent this from happening.

Often these bullies are motivated by their desire to hurt others. And they seek to hurt others to look stronger and more superior in the eyes of their peers, whom they want to impress. The bullies are showing hatred, one of the Three Poisons or G.A.S.

Hatred is a sign that they are not truly happy with themselves. Hatred is a sign that they don't have confidence and are unhappy. And some of them don't like themselves. So, in a way, we can feel somewhat sorry for them.

However, that does not mean that we can allow bullying to persist. So, you should do what you can to find ways to stop the bullying, but do not try to resolve this all *by yourself*, since you may become the target of their bullying yourself. Share what you saw and heard with the appropriate teachers or school administrators because it's their job to deal with the bullying.

In the end, in all your efforts to deal with the problem, do keep in mind the well-known spirit of the Buddha in dealing with bullying and other forms of hurtful action. And that spirit is found in the following words, "Hatred is not overcome by hatred; only by abandoning hatred can hatred be overcome." This means that meeting hatred with hatred is not the Buddhist way. So, even though we may not be able to get rid of hatred completely, we should strive to feel compassion for the victims and even for those doing the bullying.

Uncertain About My Future Work
An eighteen-year-old's story

> I soon need to decide what kind of work I want to do for my career. Unfortunately, I don't know what I want to do or know what I'm good at. Half of my friends are in the same boat, but the other half seem to have a pretty good idea what they want to do.

As you say, there are many others who are in the same boat, so please know that you are not alone. I, too, was not sure what I wanted to do when I was your age. So, in my freshman year of college, my tentative major was Business Administration, quite far from where I ended up, a Buddhist minister and scholar! A young Buddhist leader echoed this view as follows:

"I would emphasize that nothing is set in stone. Everything is always changing, i.e. impermanence. You will probably always have the opportunity to change what you do. It may be a more difficult path, but it is still an option. I knew many people who thought they knew what they wanted to do and changed during college to something completely different."[90]

What I can say on this issue will not be anything special, but one thing that is clear is that you are still young and can afford to change and grow. That is the strength of being young. If you are earnest, diligent and honest

---

90   Jason Yokoyama, an active member of the Young Adult Buddhist Association of Seattle Betsuin Buddhist Temple.

with yourself, I am confident that you will find the right work for you.

Whatever you end up doing, it would be great if you can remember the Buddhist spirit of being of *benefit* to others in your work. We need to work to pay our bills, but the work will be more meaningful if you can be of benefit to others. In life, we often gain more when we "give" to others than when we "receive" from others.

This should be the time in your life when you can explore different things. If you plan to go to college, you should utilize the first two years to fully explore various fields. Outside the classroom, you can get involved in various activities or part-time work that draws your interest.

As previously emphasized in our discussion of the quality of uniqueness related to Indra's Net of Jewels, you must be true to what interests *you* and what is in keeping with *your* abilities. It's important to hear what others, especially your parents, have to say, since they have more life experience and have your welfare in mind. However, needless to say, in the end it should be your decision.

I'm Afraid of Death But Can't Talk Aboout It With Anyone
A sixteen-year-old male's story

> Ever since I can remember, I have feared death. It's not only my own death but also those of my parents, my sister and the rest of my family that I worry about. One night a few years ago, I suddenly had this enormous anxiety attack because of my worries about death. That night I couldn't sleep at all. And I can't talk about this even with my parents or close friends because I feel I am being overly sensitive and even a bit weird.

I fully understand your experience, because I felt the same way when I was about the same age as you. Actually, there are *many* people—more than you think—who experience anxiety about death. So, you and I are not alone. And you aren't being "weird."

Actually, the Buddha and many other Buddhist masters throughout the centuries began their spiritual search motivated by a similar kind of experience as yours and mine. (See p. 44) It is because they had such strong fears that they made a commitment to find a solution to their fear and anxiety. In so doing, they came to realize things that made them feel extremely fortunate and happy, which Buddhists call "Awakening."

So, Buddhism is a religion that addresses the fear of death *head on*. Some people may consider that to be pessimistic and overly concerned with the dark side of life. I, however, don't think so. I feel grateful that there is a religion, one that has lasted for over 2,600 years, which addresses the kind of anxiety and fear that we share.

After all, everyone dies. So it is not anything we can avoid. It's natural. Because we are born, we have to die! (See a humourous take on this, p. 193)* Again, I am thankful that there is a religion like Buddhism that addresses this issue honestly and openly.

So, do check out Buddhism and practice it sincerely and consistently. I believe that such effort will clearly lead to some form of positive resolution and help you to reduce your fears and anxieties about death. The proof can be seen in the millions of Buddhists past and present who have done so!

Inferiority Complex
A seventeen-year-old female's story

> I can't talk about this even to my closest friends because, well, I feel so uneasy about it. I look at my classmates and many of them are, frankly, much prettier and smarter than me. My friend Kaci is really pretty and always has boys who are interested in her. And my other friend Jocelyn gets the best grades in class, and she doesn't even study much for the tests. I know that I shouldn't compare myself with others, but sometimes I can't help it.

Again, you are not alone in comparing yourself with others. A recent survey showed that over 80 percent of 15-year-olds experience feelings of inferiority. That is how virtually all of us are wired because our society fosters that tendency. So, you are not alone in comparing yourself with others and feeling inferior or lacking in worth.

On the other hand, you should know that you will inevitably and always feel inferior when you base your self-worth and self-identity on *comparing* yourself with others. This is because there will always be people whom you feel are superior to you in terms of abilities and appearance.

Further, most people have some level of inferiority complex. This is true even with those you envy, including Kaci and Jocelyn. I am sure that they, too, compare themselves with others. You might be surprised to find out that they, too, feel a similar sense of inferiority as you do. But you should not find comfort in knowing that, for you need to go *beyond* this and develop confidence in yourself as you are.

What should you do? The answer is the same as in other situations, which is to find the jewel within you. The answer is to establish your identity not based on comparing yourself with others. Instead, you will need to come to realize the unique jewel that you have within you and allow that jewel to shine forth in the way that makes you feel most comfortable. Only you can determine what that looks like, because it will be determined by what you like and what you are good at.

In my case, I was fortunate to find my jewel within, a profession and way of life with which I felt comfortable. However, it took quite some time to come to that realization and to overcome a heavy burden of inferiority.

Let me explain in detail. I was born in Japan, but when I was 10 years old my American-born mother decided to return to the United States, and my Japan-born father was in favour of this move. So, my entire family moved to what is now Silicon Valley in Northern California. My brothers and I spoke no English and our life in our new home turned out to be more difficult than the one we had known in our upper middle-class lifestyle in Japan.

So, I felt inferior since I could not speak English at all. Plus, I was an ethnic (Asian) and a religious (Buddhist) minority in a strange land. Fortunately, my classmates and teachers were good to me, so that was a saving grace. But I was teased as being an "FOB" (fresh off the boat immigrant) by a fellow Japanese American. So, I felt inferior to even my fellow Japanese Americans who were born in America and whose families were well established in America. And they, of course, spoke English perfectly.

However, my sense of inferiority began to weaken greatly when I began to learn more about my religion and my culture. At the Buddhist temple, I became a Sunday school teacher assistant when I was in high school and began to gain more pride in being a Buddhist as I learned more about the history and teachings of Buddhism. In college, I majored in Cultural Anthropology and focused on Japanese culture, which increased my appreciation of my cultural roots. So, the knowledge I gained gave me confidence in my religion and culture, which were reasons for being proud of who I am.

Furthermore, the fact that I spoke Japanese till age 10 provided me with an advantage over others who wanted to study the language. I, then, developed proficiency in Japanese language to a point whereby I eventually was able to carry out the necessary studies to qualify as a priest and a scholar of Buddhism. So, this is the case of my being able to turn what once seemed to be a disadvantage into an advantage.

I realize that your situation is different from mine, but the solution is generally the same for everyone. As I mentioned in the beginning, we all need to keep in mind the dangers of comparing ourselves with others. Instead, you are encouraged to develop the strengths and qualities that are part of you, and to aim for something you like and are good at. This may require you to take what you thought was a weakness and turn it into your strength.

You can surely do it. Out of the mud grows a lotus flower! (See p. 105)

11 Questions Often Asked about Buddhism

THESE ANSWERS are meant to help you to respond to questions from others in a concise and direct manner. Where there is more information available in this book, page or chapter numbers are provided.

Buddhism as a Religion

What is Buddhism? Buddhism is a world religion, the followers of which aspire to be like the Buddha, who some 2,600 years ago awakened to truth to overcome suffering for everyone. (See p. 46)

Is Buddhism a religion or philosophy? In the beginning at the time of Shakyamuni Buddha, he taught his disciples the way to cultivate themselves to attain Awakening. So, Buddhism could not fit within the usual definition of "religion" or "philosophy."

So, Buddhism is not a religion? Some people say it is *not* a religion because it does not speak of a God, who is all-knowing, all-powerful and the creator of everything. On the other hand, it *is* a religion because it includes faith, rituals and practices and is of "ultimate importance" to many of its followers.

If so, is Buddhism not a philosophy then? It does include teachings that are philosophical, intellectual or rational in nature like the Four Noble Truths. However, because Buddhism also includes faith, ethics and meditation, it is more than just philosophy.

Why is Buddhism a "world religion"? Though it is concentrated in Asia, Buddhists are now found in many parts of the world, including North America, Europe and Oceania. (See Chapters 1, 5)

What are the other major world religions? They are Christianity with 2.3 billion followers and Islam with 1.8 billion followers. Buddhists number 500 million followers.

Which of the three is the oldest? Buddhism is the oldest, having begun around 500 BCE, while Christianity started around the beginning of the Common Era and Islam around 650 CE.

Why isn't Hinduism considered a "world" religion? It has more followers (1.1 billion) than Buddhism (500 million) but is confined mostly to one country or cultural sphere, the Indian subcontinent.

Buddhas and Awakened People

Can humans become Buddha? Buddha means "an awakened person." Shakyamuni Buddha was a human being born in Nepal-India and became a "Buddha" when he attained Awakening at age thirty-five. (See p. 46)

What does "Buddha" mean? In Sanskrit, it means "an awakened person," who has become freed from suffering. The aim of many Buddhists is to become Buddhas themselves.

Who are Bodhisattvas? They refer to 1) those who are serious seekers of Awakening, or 2) persons who have attained high levels of Awakening and dedicate themselves to leading others to Awakening.

What do you become awakened to? One example is the Four Marks of Life, which are, Life 1) "is a bumpy road," 2) "is interdependent," 3) "is impermanent," and 4) "can be great." (See Ch. 8)

What happens when you become more awakened? You become more joyful, generous, compassionate, curious, energetic and at peace with oneself, and less swayed by your own greed, anger/hatred and stupidity or G.A.S.

What are the qualities that awakened persons come to possess? They feel a profound love and compassion for living beings, treat all people equally, and feel a deep bond with all living beings and with nature.

Teachings

Do you have a holy book like the Bible or Koran? Yes, it is called "sutras," which contain mostly the teachings spoken by the Buddha. The sutras, however, do not fit into one book, for they amount to many books.

What is Karma? It doesn't mean fate or punishment but instead points to *our actions*: what we think, what we say and what we do. Karma nurtures our mind so that we can experience a deeper sense of happiness, satisfaction and gratitude than most people. (See p. 88)

So, Karma doesn't mean fate or punishment? No, it does not. So, many Americans are using it incorrectly. Plus, Karma should not *always* be thought of as bad or negative, because if we act in accord with Buddhism that becomes a good and positive Karma.

So, Karma determines the quality of our mind and feelings? Yes, the more we think, speak and act in keeping with the Buddhist teachings, we become not only happier but also more self-assured and confident.

Can Karma make you become more popular and successful in life? Karma (as how we think and act) cannot *guarantee* this but can certainly increase the chance of your becoming more popular and successful because people will find you trustworthy and want to associate with you.

Did the Buddha believe in reincarnation? He accepted it as an established worldview of his time but did not consider it as *mandatory* for the purpose of realizing Awakening.

Do you pray? Yes, we pray in the sense of wishing peace and happiness for others and ourselves, but not for worldly benefits such as material things.

But some Buddhists do pray for worldly benefits, don't they? That is true, but they are not being true to the original teachings of the Buddha.

Schools, Denominations and Traditions

How many kinds of Buddhism are there? Two. They are Theravada (school of the elders) and Mahayana (larger vehicle). Theravada is found mostly in Southeast Asia and Mahayana in East Asia. Some consider Vajrayana (diamond or thunderbolt vehicle) as the third kind, but most scholars include it under Mahayana. (See p. 53)

Which city in the world has the largest number of Buddhist schools? It is the Los Angeles metropolitan area, with about 100 different kinds of Buddhist schools, followed closely by these North American metropolises: Vancouver, Honolulu, the San Francisco Bay Area, Seattle, Chicago, Toronto, and New York.

What is common to all schools? People in all the schools of Buddhism take refuge in the Three Gems or Treasures, which are Buddha (awakened person), Dharma (teachings) and Sangha (community of teachers and fellow Buddhists).

Other Religions

What about the salvation of people of other religions? We would never say that they would not be saved because we believe that all *true* religions can lead their followers to their destination.

Do Buddhists believe in God? "Yes," if "God" refers to truth and compassion (or love), but "no" if God is a creator of the universe and the judge of our actions.

You don't call it "God," do you? No, we call it "Dharma," which means "teachings" but also the "ultimate reality or truth" at the foundation of the teachings.

What is the main difference between Buddhism and Judaism, Christianity, and Islam? Buddhists do not believe in a God who created human beings and the universe. So, we can more easily accept the scientific explanation of how the universe began and functions.

Do Buddhists celebrate Christmas? Most North American Buddhists celebrate it as a national holiday that promotes the spirit of sharing and goodwill, which Buddhists also value highly.

Wouldn't that be unfaithful to the Buddhist religion? We don't feel that, for we believe it is important to see beyond *form* to appreciate the *spirit*, which we also share.

Misconceptions about Buddhism

Isn't Buddhism pessimistic? No, it isn't pessimistic. Although the Buddhist teachings address our "suffering," they lead us to Awakening in which one becomes calm, joyful, thoughtful and optimistic.

I've heard that awakened people come to have no feelings and take no interest in life. Is this true? That is not correct, since the Buddha acutely felt the suffering of others and spent 45 years sharing his wisdom so that others could be truly happy in the same way that he became happy. (See p. 48)

So, Buddhists are not detached or indifferent toward the world? That's right, because one of the main reasons for the success of the early Buddhist religion was its desire and ability to respond to the needs of the community.

But Pope John Paul II said, "The 'enlightenment' experienced by Buddha comes down to the conviction that the world is bad, that it is the source of evil and suffering for man."[91] We believe that Pope John Paul II has not understood correctly because the source of suffering is not the *world*. Correctly understood, the source of suffering is our personal attachments or G.A.S., which are greed, anger/hatred and stupidity.

So, Buddhism doesn't believe that the world is bad? No, the world is neither all positive nor all negative, for it is what it is! So, whether the world is good or bad depends on how we see it and how we interact with it. "With my mind, I *make* the world" is what the Buddha said, as is recorded in the famous *Dhammapada* passage.

It seems that Buddhism only cares about the mind. It's true that Buddhism is subjective or psychological in nature, but the goal is to transform the mind toward the goal of a happier, wiser and more compassionate self, which then can contribute to a more peaceful and happier world.

Why Buddhism?

What points about Buddhism do you like? There are several points. Buddhism does not believe that it's the *only* way and accepts other long-surviving religions as valid paths to peace and happiness.

What is another point you like about Buddhism? I like that we can fully accept the scientific view about how the world began and to maintain the spirit of curiosity about the social and natural world.

Any others? Yes. Buddha said, "All sentient beings possess Buddha nature." This means that not only humans, but animals, birds, fish, and other creatures are all sacred.

But we eat other living beings, don't we? Yes, we, too, need to live, but we

---

91 John Paul II, *Crossing the Threshold of Hope*. (Alfred A. Knopf, 1994, p. 85).

partake of them with deep gratitude for their sacrifice; one of the ways to show our gratitude is by not leaving any leftovers.

What is another point you like about Buddhism? I like that it's not a "sin" if people don't take interest in the Buddhist teaching. If people are not interested, we simply wait for them to become interested.

You don't do anything but just wait? No, we do make every effort to make the teachings available to others in the belief that they will take interest when conditions become ripe within their lives.

Are there any other reasons for being attracted to Buddhism? I like the emphasis on *personal* understanding. This means that we do not accept the Dharma unquestioningly, but only if it makes sense personally in our daily lives.

So, did the Buddha really encourage that? Yes, he taught, "Do not accept a statement because it's found in our books, nor because it's supposed to be 'acceptable,' nor because your teacher said so." He recommended that people take the teachings and consider them and put their insights and learning to the test in their own lives.

It sounds like "anything goes" and Buddhists can do anything they wish. No, we don't do whatever we please, for the standard is the Dharma (teachings), and ethics are a very strong part of the Buddhist teachings and practices. However, these ethical recommendations are guidelines, not divine commandments. The Buddha wanted us to test the Dharma in our lives before accepting it.

Any other reasons for liking Buddhism? I am also impressed by how relatively peaceful Buddhism has been throughout its history. "Religious wars" among its denominations have been few and far between.

12 Buddhist Humour as a Way to Learn and Share Buddhism

WE HAVE STRESSED THE IMPORTANCE of humour in this book as seen in the way it has been incorporated into the explanation of the teachings. This chapter includes new ones as well as all of the humourous and light-hearted entries that have appeared previously in this book. I have done so even though some readers may think it redundant, since I wanted all humours to be collected in *one* section with fuller comments *not* found previously.

The entries are divided into five categories: Teachings; The Character of Buddhism; Puns and Plays on Words; Awakened People; as well as Misunderstandings and Slip-ups.

Teachings

Buddha and the Vacuum Cleaner

A: Why couldn't the Buddha vacuum clean under the sofa?
B: I don't know. Why?
A: Well, it's because he had no *attachments*!
(See p. 80 for its cartoon)

Comment: "Attachments," such as clinging to the idea that our team has to always win, are a cause of our suffering. As an awakened or enlightened person who no longer suffers, Buddha doesn't have any attachments because he has overcome or gotten rid of them. Of course, "attachments" has another meaning when it comes to vacuum cleaners! (See pp. 88, 92, 93 for more on attachment)*

Email Attachment 1

DISCIPLE: Master, may I be permitted to send emails?
BUDDHIST TEACHER: Yes, only if you do not have any

attachments![92]

Comment: As in the above, the aim of Buddhists is to overcome or reduce attachments. Unfortunately, as in the above, the Master has the wrong understanding of "attachment" as it applies to email.

Email Attachment 2

> EMAIL FRIEND: You said there would be an attachment to the last mail you sent me, but I don't see it.
> ME: Oh, sorry about that. I was just trying to be a good Buddhist. No *attachments!*[93]

Comment: I will actually use this as an excuse whenever I forget to send an attachment as promised. However, I know that I shouldn't use my religion to justify my failure!

A Monk and a Hot Dog

A Buddhist monk wanted a hot dog, so he went to a hot dog food stall.

> VENDOR: "What would you like, sir?"
> MONK: "Make me *one* with *everything*!"

After getting the hot dog and giving the vendor a $20 bill, the monk did not get his change after waiting for over a minute. Finally, the monk asked, a bit flustered…

> MONK: Where, where…is my change?
> VENDOR (pointing his finger at the monk): Sir, the *change* must come from *within you*!

Comment: In my opinion, this is one of the best Buddhist jokes. I refer you to my earlier explanation and the wonderful cartoon). (See p. 82)

---

92 From Mr. Deuce Nakano, via email on November 14, 2015.

93 I wish to acknowledge that this joke is based on a greeting card of the same theme. However, our wording is a bit different, and the cartoon is original.

Buddhist R&B Musicians

Q: Why are there no Buddhist Rhythm & Blues musicians?
B: I don't know.
A: That's because the Buddhists got no *soul*!

Comment: This also involves an insight into the nature of our reality, which the Buddha expressed as "Life is interdependent" or "nothing exists on its own." (See p. 100) So for Buddhists, a person does not exist completely on his or her own or a person has no essence that is completely independent and permanent. However, some people have misunderstood this to mean that Buddhists do not believe in a "soul."

In this joke, however, "soul" is used in a different way: the musician's *spirit* and *sense of style* needed to play Rhythm & Blues music. So, the humour comes from the two different meanings of the word "soul": 1) permanent essence of a person; and 2) musical sense of style and spirit. This joke insinuates that Buddhists don't have a soul in the *second* meaning, when the fact of the matter is that Buddhists don't have a soul in the *first* meaning.

Finally, as we see in this book, Awakened Buddhists also have "soul" in the second meaning: a caring, lively spirit for life itself, so definitely for music as well!

Buddhist Medical Examiner Gets Fired

There was a medical examiner, who happened to be a very devout Buddhist. He tried to live his religion faithfully in his life. One day he was fired from his job as the county medical examiner.

The reason he lost his job was that he wrote down the same reason as the cause of death on every one of the death certificates he issued. Rather than the usual common causes of death, such as heart failure and stroke, he wrote down the same reason: *birth*!

Comment: In other words, this doctor's thinking is that "we die because we are *born*." If we hadn't been born, we would not have to die. Unfortunately, he took his religion too seriously and zealously applied it to his work as a medical examiner. As a doctor, he should have found the specific medical cause of death instead of inappropriately applying his religious belief.

This joke can be better appreciated if we understand the doctor's outlook, which is based on the Buddhist teaching of *transmigration* or the "cycle of birth and death" (in Hinduism, "reincarnation"). The aim of Buddhism is to be liberated from transmigration or the cycle of birth and death by becoming Awakened, which means the person will no longer have to be born and go through this unending cycle. In other words, "no birth" results in "no death."

It should be pointed out that a belief in transmigration existed before Buddhism and was adopted by Buddhists as a common worldview when Buddhism got started. In my view, it does not constitute the *central* teaching of Buddhism, so a belief in the literal meaning of "reincarnation" is not required to be a Buddhist. In fact, many Buddhists today do not take it literally but instead understand it more symbolically.

Cliff Hanger

A man is on the edge of a cliff hanging on for dear life. The Buddha appears, and the man looks up and says with his last ounce of energy, "Oh Buddha…save me…please save me!"

The Buddha replies, "I will…. Let go!"

Comment: The man thought he was on a cliff, and that the ground was a *hundred* metres below. However, he was actually only *one* metre above the ground!

This is a metaphor for how we mistakenly think that when things don't go our way or when we feel that we are in trouble, "It's the end of the world!" But from the Buddha's point of view, we are often greatly exaggerating our difficulties. We are "making a mountain out of a molehill!" The Buddha wanted the man to realize that he was fine, because the ground was only three feet below him.

For example, say your team has lost a very important game by a narrow margin. It's devastating for you and your teammates, and you may feel as if you fell a hundred metres. You had all practiced so hard and came so close to winning. But in the big scheme of things, losing a big game in this way happens to all teams, sooner or later. So, the Buddha is admonishing you, "It's no big deal. Let go!"

River Crossing

A Zen Buddhist master and his student come to a river, and there they find a young lady who wants to get across the river. But the current might be too strong for her to wade across it, so she is debating whether or not to try to cross on her own; she doesn't know quite what to do.

Seeing her hesitation and judging that it would be dangerous for this young woman to cross the river by herself, the Zen master offers to help. After she accepts his offer, the master carries her in his arms and manages to wade across the river. Once they reach the other bank, he puts her down. The young lady thanks the master, and they go their separate ways.

The master and the student head toward their destination, but the student monk is extremely bothered that his teacher has broken the rule of conduct that advises monks not to touch women. However, he can't quite muster up enough courage to confront his teacher. Finally, after they had walked several kilometres, the student, visibly upset and no longer able to hold back his feelings, finally blurts out, "Teacher, wasn't that a violation of the monastic regulation forbidding you from coming in physical contact with a woman? You even *held* her to carry her across the river!"

The master then calmly replies, "Well, I put her down way back there. It seems you are the one who is still *holding on* to her. Why haven't *you* put her down yet?"

Comment: The disciple is hung up on the rules, which are important during training, but are not meant to do away with common sense, compassion, and helpfulness. Rather, the teacher is motivated by a higher standard of thought and action and motivated by compassion to assist those who are in need, like the young lady.

Appearance of Things

Things are not what they seem, ...nor are they *otherwise*!
(*Lankavatara Sutra*)

Comment: This may be a little hard to appreciate because this line is meant to discourage us from having *set* or *fixed* views and opinions about things.

For example, we all harbor opinions about our friends as being this or that, but that may not be the complete picture, for we don't know *everything* about each of our friends. Our opinion is based on a limited perspective, for we know him or her as a friend but not as a son or daughter or brother or sister.

Further, our opinion about a person often depends on how we are feeling. If we are tired and grumpy, we tend to have a negative opinion of the people we meet. So, it would be good to remind ourselves, "They are not [ultimately or always] what they seem [to me]."

Then, what does the *latter* phrase (in the sutra passage) "nor are they otherwise" mean? For example, we thought [say, a person by the name of] Tom is short-tempered, but the *first* part of the passage cautioned us against thinking that Tom is always and by nature short-tempered. So, we come to think that he is *not* short-tempered.

But since the second half of the sutra passage says, "nor are they otherwise," we should also *not* cling to the opinion that "he is *not* short-tempered" either. This means we should not cling to either one view or the other.

You may be quite confused by now. Well, what is important to get from this sutra passage is that all views and opinions are limited. They are relative and are not absolute. So, we should not get too "hung up" or insist on them as *absolutely* or *always* correct. Buddhism encourages us to be flexible, pliable and open to other possible views and opinions.

Finally, if all views are relative and conditioned, does this mean we *shouldn't* have values or opinions? No, that is not what is being said. To the contrary, values and opinions are important in living our daily lives. However, the sutra passage is simply saying that we should be flexible in our views and be *open* to other possibilities because our own understanding is most likely not always complete or comprehensive.

The Character of Buddhism

Here and Now!

A Christian guy is carrying a placard on a busy city sidewalk that reads: "Jesus is coming!"
Then behind him there is a Buddhist, smiling and carrying a placard of his own that reads: "Buddha, here NOW!"

Comment: According to the Christian doctrine of the "second coming of Jesus," Jesus will return to this world in the *future*. Here, the Buddhist is making a contrast by emphasizing one of its main teachings, to live in the here and *now*. I like the fact that the Buddhist is smiling and playful. (See p. 7 for cartoon)

The Emperor and a Buddhist Master

The emperor asked Master Guandao, "What happens to a man of Awakening after death?"

"Why would I know?" replied Guandao.
"Because you are a master," answered the emperor.
"Yes I am, your majesty," said Guandao, "but not a *dead* one!"

Comment: Master Guandao's response is meant to show that Buddhism is mostly concerned with becoming Awakened in *this* very life. After becoming Awakened, one no longer worries or is concerned about what happens after death because he is very much at peace with himself in the here and now.

Buddhist Blessings

STEPHEN: Can you bless my new car?
BUDDHIST PRIEST: What benefits do you hope to get from a blessing?
STEPHEN: I don't want anything bad to happen to my brand-new car.
BUDDHIST PRIEST: We don't usually do blessings, since they might be understood as a form of magic, and this goes against our teachings. But if you really insist, I shall do it as a *pastoral* service to give you some peace of mind.

(A few weeks later, Stephen returns, very upset, to tell the priest that the car was stolen, insinuating that the blessing had failed.)

BUDDHIST PRIEST: I'm very sorry to hear this, but the blessing I gave doesn't work for *stolen* cars; it works only to prevent the car from getting into an accident!

Comment: The priest felt obliged out of compassion to help Stephen enjoy peace of mind about his car, at least for a while. Stephen, like many people, saw religion only as a means for worldly benefits.

Buddhism in its original form did not believe in these types of spells and blessings. However, as Buddhism became a religion for the large population, some groups responded to their members' worldly needs.

At its core, Buddhism helps us to cultivate our mind in order to be able to respond positively and without much suffering when things do not go our way. I hope that through this experience Stephen will become interested in pursuing the *true purpose* of Buddhism. (See p. 87 for further discussion based on this.)

Psychic Power

Someone had spent a long time meditating in order to have the psychic power of walking on water.

The Buddha said to him: "Why don't you just cross the river on the ferry?"

Comment: This shows that the aim of Buddhism is not to develop psychic power but to train us to develop greater wisdom and compassion to reduce suffering and increase happiness for oneself and for others. Buddhism is primarily not concerned with extraordinary powers or miracles.

Happy Meal

A: Why do some Buddhists like to buy the Happy Meal whenever they go to McDonald's?
B: I don't have a clue.
A: Because the First Noble Truth points out, "We all experience unhappiness."

Comment: I must admit this joke isn't the best, but it does help to make an important point. In any religion, there are members who don't fully understand the teachings of their own religion. These Buddhists are a good example. Only by *changing* our views about life can we overcome unhappiness.

Buying things will never help us to become *truly* happy, of course! A "Happy Meal," as I am using in the joke, is a symbol of materialism, which includes the belief that owning things will bring us happiness. Buddhists understand that we need a certain amount of material comfort but believe that *true* happiness comes from how you *experience* life, not what material things you *acquire* in life.

Land of Smiles

A: You probably have heard that Thailand, a strong Buddhist country, is known as the "land of smiles," right?
B: Yeah, I have.
A: Did you know that Thai Buddhists don't ride on motorcycles in Thailand?
B: Why is that?
A: It's because when these happy smiling Buddhists ride their

motorcycles, bugs can fly into their mouths and get stuck between their teeth!

Comment: I first heard this from a group of lay Catholics at an interreligious gathering in Rome. So, I adapted this to the Thai Buddhists whom I met back in 1970, when I became a novice monk at a monastery there. The Thai people did seem to be generally very happy. I attributed that to their Buddhist faith. But as with my Catholic friends, I believe that any true religion can help people to lead a happier life.

Puns and Plays on Words

G.A.S. for the Three Poisons

G.A.S. stands for Greed, Anger/hatred and Stupidity.

Comment: This usage of catchy acronyms may not be humourous in the traditional sense, but I think it is a fun and light-hearted way of learning and remembering the teachings. G.A.S. represents the causes of suffering. So, I often say in my classes, the aim of Buddhism is to *release gas*, but please just don't do it here and now!

I actually prefer "Aversion" over "Anger/hatred," because the meaning of the word "Aversion" can include both Anger and Hatred.

D.A.I. for the Three Poisons

D.A.I. stands for Desire, Aversion and Ignorance

Comment: This is another acronym for the Three Poisons, which is pronounced "die." It's saying that if we become overwhelmed by D.A.I., we will die *spiritually* and *mentally*.

G.A.F. for the Three Poisons

Yet another acronym for the Three Poisons is G.A.F.

Comment: This stands for greed, aversion or anger, and foolishness. So, when we think, speak, and act influenced by G.A.F., we are prone to commit a lot of *gaffs*.

Remembering the Four Marks of Existence and Their Opposites

"Think BIIG and don't think SMAL!"

Comment: This has helped many to remember this important Buddhist teaching, making use of a popular phrase, "Think Big!" (See p. 128 for a detailed explanation)*

Remembering the Eightfold Noble Path

To remember this teaching, think of a Mr. V.I. SCLEMM.

Comment: I heard this many years ago from a senior priest, who in his sermon provided this as a way to remember all eight aspects of the Eightfold Noble Path. He said to think of a German name, Mr. V.I. SCLEMM (pronounced "Shlem"); for example, "V" stands for "View" and "I" stands for "Intention" and so on! I initially thought it was funny but a bit silly, but in the many years since then it has helped *me* to remember the eight. The senior priest has passed on, but whenever I talk about the Eightfold Noble Path, Mr. V. I. SCLEMM pops up in my mind with a warm feeling for this teaching and for the senior priest who shared it with us. (See p. 83)

Shoes

Drs. Sunnan Kubose, Alfred Bloom and Kenneth Tanaka were serving as panelists at a summer study session held at the Buddhist Study Center in Honolulu. Dr. Kubose spoke passionately about doing Gassho, which means to put our palms together as an expression of gratitude.

He then spoke specifically about doing Gassho to our "shoes" because they are taken for granted and are always being stepped on and not appreciated. Then, these impromptu comments followed:

BLOOM: Dr. Kubose, your spirit goes to the *soul* of our tradition!
TANAKA: Yes, it's a *shoe in* for the best humour of the summer session!
A VOICE FROM THE AUDIENCE: Yes, we should always put our *best foot* forward!

Comment: Please don't *cringe*, for it really went over well *then*! Humour is best when we actually experience it. Nevertheless, these puns aren't *that* bad, are they?

Root Canal Treatment

A: Why did a Buddhist refuse Novocaine during a root canal?
B: I don't know. Why?
A: He wanted to *transcend dental medication.*

Comment: The line "transcend dental medication" is a play on word for "transcendental meditation," which is actually a non-Buddhist form of meditation commonly known as "TM," which stands for Transcendental Meditation.

Awakened People or Those Approaching Awakening

The Dalai Lama's Birthday Present

It's the Dalai Lama's birthday. He is surrounded by a group of his top disciples who stand near him, looking pleased with the present they have just handed him. The Dalai Lama is very happy as he looks down into the bag holding his present.

However, apparently there is *no present* in the bag, and the Dalai Lama exclaims, "Wow, this is just what I always wanted… emptiness!"

Comment: "Emptiness" refers to the truth that everything arises and exists by depending on other things. So there is nothing that arises and exists completely on *its own*, which if it did exist would be called "own-nature." Another way of explaining this truth is to say, "All things are *empty* of such own-nature." However, it takes deep wisdom after an enormous amount of study and practice to realize this truth. That is why it's something that even the Dalai Lama deeply cherishes.

In this humourous scene, the Dalai Lama finds that the bag was *empty* because it didn't contain a birthday present. There was nothing in it. So, he wisely makes a joke out of it by purposely using the same word, *emptiness*, which—as explained above—refers to a deep Buddhist insight.

I love the Dalai Lama's sense of humour, a quality that is found in people who are either Awakened or very much on the way to Awakening.

Past Life

AMERICAN INTERVIEWER: I must ask you this question. You are the fourteenth in the succession of reincarnated Dalai Lamas, who have died and were reborn. Do you remember anything from your past life?

DALAI LAMA: Do I remember my past life? Mmm.... To tell the truth, these days, I don't even remember what I did *yesterday*!

Comment: This actually took place on an American TV show called "Nightline" at the end of an interview that a well-known journalist Ted Koppel did with the Dalai Lama. Reincarnation reflects a long and enduring tradition, which cannot be done justice to by a simple question on a TV show in front of two million viewers. So, the Dalai Lama wisely responded with humour. After this, the interviewer Ted Koppel realized how inappropriate his question was, and he then turned red in the face out of embarrassment and apologized profusely.

Briefly, the tradition of a reincarnated Dalai Lama is several hundred years old. In this belief system, Tibetan Buddhists believe that their most highly ranked Tibetan monk, the Dalai Lama, is reborn after he dies. Then, in this tradition, a search was initiated throughout Tibet to find that child, who then is educated and trained to become the next Dalai Lama.

Satori Awakening

This is quoted from a description of a conversation between Shunryu Suzuki, a Zen master and the founder of the San Francisco Zen Center, and Huston Smith, a famous scholar of world religions. Prof. Smith says:

"When, four months before his death, I had the opportunity to ask him why satori didn't figure in his book, his wife leaned toward me and whispered impishly, 'It's because he hasn't had it,' whereupon the [Suzuki] Roshi batted his fan at her in mock consternation and with finger to his lips hissed, 'Shhhh! Don't tell him!'"

"When our laughter had subsided, he said simply, 'It's not that satori is unimportant, but it's not the part of Zen that needs to be stressed.'"[94]

Comment: Satori refers to Awakening in Zen Buddhism. Suzuki Roshi had experienced satori, and because of it he attracted hundreds of capable and dedicated disciples and was able to initiate one of the largest and most vibrant centres of Buddhism in North America.

People who have experienced satori are extremely humble and feel no need to "show off." They often have a playful sense of humour, as we see in the way he responded to his wife's comment by saying, "Shhh! Don't tell him!"

Misunderstandings or Slip-ups!

Praying

Three men go fishing in a small boat in a huge lake 20 miles wide. Suddenly, the boat capsizes in the middle of the lake, but the men manage to hang on to the capsized boat. They want to swim to the shore, but it is just too far away.

So, one of them says, "Well, guys, we got no choice but to pray to God." He then says to one of the other two men, "So, you *pray*." That man answers, "I'm an atheist, so I don't believe in God." So then, they turn to the other guy, who replies, "I'm a Buddhist, and we have Buddha who is a spiritual *teacher* but not God."

Frustrated, the first guy says, "OK then, I guess I have to do it. I don't go to church, but I live next door to one, so I hear them *praying* all the time. I think I can remember the prayer,

"O69... B5... I21... G40..."

Comment: Bingo games are popular activities as well as an important source of income at many churches and religious institutions, including the Buddhist temple in California that I served as minister for three years. What is hilarious is that this guy mistook the calling out of the Bingo letters and numbers for prayer!

---

94 This story by Prof. Huston Smith is found in the preface of the well-known book by Shunryu Suzuki, *Zen Mind, Beginner's Mind* (Weatherhill, 1970), p. 9.

Oneness

A highly respected pioneer Buddhist priest in Chicago, Rev. Gyomay Kubose, loved the word "Oneness," which referred to ultimate truth. So, he often signed his books by writing "Oneness" next to his name. One day, he mistakenly wrote a wrong letter in the word, which made it sound hilarious.

He had written "Onemess"!

Comment: I can't adequately explain why I find this humourous. It's probably because as this highly respected senior priest tries to express the ultimate truth (Oneness), but just a small error (between an "n" and an "m") ends up expressing something exactly the opposite (One mess)!

My Face in Buddha

Many Jodo Shinshu Buddhists in North America grew up with priests or ministers from Japan who did not speak English well. One third-generation Japanese American recalls how as a child he could not understand what his minister was saying when he led them in reciting the "Three Treasures" for he would say:

"I *putto* my *face* in Buddha, I *putto* my *face* in Dharma, I *putto* my *face* in Sangha."

So, the young boy wondered, "Do I put my face in Buddha?" Does this mean, "I kiss the Buddha?" He was confused.

The correct pronunciation was, "I *put* my *faith* in Buddha."

Comment: It is not my intent to make fun of the minister's English, for I appreciate the hardship that Buddhist priests from Asia faced as they strove to share the Dharma in North America. They had to adjust to a new culture and learn to speak English well enough to talk about a difficult subject. For those Japanese priests who grew up in the 1930s and during the Second World War, when English was not taught in schools in Japan because English was considered an "enemy language," fluency in English came much slower. They tried hard, but some still had difficulty with pronunciation.

By the way, that young boy is now a respected Buddhist priest. It could be that his "confusion" may have helped him to question and deepen his appreciation of the teachings, which made him want to learn more and to eventually become a priest! So, confusion and doubt can be good and might be better than disinterest or apathy, because the former indicates that you are *interested*.

A Misunderstanding That Motivated a Boy to Go to Sunday School

When a Japanese American Jodo Shinshu Buddhist was a little boy, he went to Sunday School, in part, because he got candies for attending. So, he thought that all those years he was "praying" for the candies during the religious service when he chanted the last line of the sutra verses (*Junirai* or *The Twelve Verses of Bowing*), which was repeated many times. That line went "*koga chorai midason*," meaning, "Thus, I bow to Amida Buddha." However, not knowing Japanese very well, all those years he was actually chanting incorrectly, "*chodai chodai kudasai*," meaning "Give me, give me, oh please give me!"

Comment: I really love this story, for it shows how the temples were an enjoyable and fun place for children. It is said the Buddha utilized numerous "skilful means" to share the teachings, so why not candies!

By the way, it worked for this little boy, for he has become a respected lay leader in the Buddhist Churches of America organization.

Dharma Debate

Once a Korean Zen monk and a Tibetan lama met for a doctrinal debate at a gathering at Harvard University as hundreds looked on. It was an impressive sight when the two eminent monks, in their flowing robes, entered the stage, attended by their disciples. The Korean Zen master began by thrusting out his arm, holding an orange. He then asked, "*What is this*?" seeking an answer, which in Zen calls for a profound spiritual understanding.

Unaccustomed to this Zen style, the Tibetan lama seemed confused and turned toward his translator. They whispered back and forth for several minutes as the hushed audience waited in great anticipation, the Tibetan translator finally addressed the crowd:

"The Master says, 'What is the matter with him? Don't they have oranges where he comes from?'"

The debate went no further![95]

Comment: Buddhism is a world religion with many different branches and denominations, many of which have never interacted with each other. However, in America where all the major schools coexist, the different traditions

---

95 Mark Epstein, *Thoughts without a Thinker: Psychotherapy from a Buddhist Perspective* (Basic Books, A Division of Harper Collins Publishers, 1995), pp. 13–14.

are able to meet for the first time and to get to know each other. This was a great opportunity for a dialogue between the Korean Zen Buddhist teacher and the Tibetan Buddhist teacher, but the outcome turned out to be anticlimactic and comical, especially the Tibetan lama's answer!

Epilogue

As we come to the end of this book, I want to leave you with three reminders.

First, please do all that you can to become truly happy in life, which is what Buddhist Awakening is about. You have many years ahead of you in life, which will bring difficulties as well as joys. However, with Dharma on your side, you will be much better able to manifest that gem within to help you deal with the difficulties that are sure to come your way.

If you are better able to deal with your difficulties, you will be a happier person. And the highest state of happiness is what we call "Awakening," which is represented by the person we call the Buddha. We do not have to be *perfectly* awakened like the Buddha. The reality is that we won't be. That's because, unlike the monks and nuns who are living in a "pristine" environment, we lead lives within the challenges of family, school, work and society. So, we have done well if we have realized even a bit of what the Buddha attained. It will be to your own benefit and for those around you to do so.

I am convinced that you will be able to realize the greater peace and happiness of Awakening if you apply and seek the Dharma with *sincerity* and *diligence* for any extended period of time. Remember that you already possess the gem inside of you, which means you simply need to allow it to shine forth.

The second of my two ending reminders is especially for those of you who consider yourself Buddhist. Unlike the time when I was growing up in the '50s and early '60s, Buddhism, as I've pointed out in this book, is now much better known and accepted by many as a religion for Canadians. Furthermore, Buddhism is one of the three major world religions and is the oldest among them.

So, there are these and many other reasons to be proud to be a Buddhist, but the best way to feel that pride is for you yourself to acquire good *knowledge* and personal *conviction* about Buddhism. I truly hope that this book has contributed even a tiny bit toward fostering in you these two goals: knowledge and conviction.

The third reminder is for you to do what you can to promote Buddhism and peace. The two are not separate. If you promote Buddhism, you will be contributing to peace.

You should, of course, not *impose* your beliefs onto others but share them with clarity and confidence when the conditions are right. Buddhists have tended to be shy about sharing and promoting their feelings and thoughts about their religion. So, *don't keep quiet* when you have an opportunity to discuss religion among your friends or at school or work. Also, if there are events at school or your workplace for personal sharing about religion, volunteer to do what you can to present your knowledge and conviction about Buddhism.

One of the reasons for promoting Buddhism is to contribute to peace in the world, not just for Buddhists but also for people of all religions and of no religion. Further, peace should not be just for human beings, it should be for all living creatures; we should not bring unnecessary harm to animals, fish, birds, and insects. As the world becomes even more interconnected and interdependent as Indra's Net of Gems reminds us, our actions will impact others near and far with much greater intensity.

This is clearly evident in the challenges we are facing with regard to climate change, for what one country does affects the rest of the world. Global warming and the rising of the sea levels have no boundaries.

Unfortunately, our generation has not done enough to stem the tide, for which I feel partly responsible and wish to apologize. I shall do whatever I can during the rest of the time that I have left on earth. So, let us, you and I, join all others who are already committed to this vital task.

This environmental issue is intimately related to the issue of peace. Needless to say, as the physical conditions worsen, we will witness and be affected by greater discord and suffering over food, water and air, leading to economic and political upheaval. Without a healthy physical environment, it will be difficult for us to realize the mental and spiritual peace that Buddhists seek. The objective outer world is intimately related to the subjective inner world. The two are not separate and both are needed for greater peace. So, please do whatever you can to promote Buddhism for the goal of personal and world peace.

> Make yourself the lamp.
> Make the teachings the lamp.
> (Buddha, *Nibbana Sutta*)

Appendices

Appendix I

Important Dates in Buddhism and Christianity

Year	Buddhism	Christianity
600 BCE	Buddha is born (ca. 566 BCE)	
300	King Ashoka takes reign (268 BCE)	
	Theravada Buddhism goes to Sri Lanka	
100	Mahayana Buddhism merges	
0 CE		Jesus of Nazareth is born
100	Buddhism goes to China (ca. 100)	
	Buddhism goes to Vietnam	
200	Nagarjuna, Mahayana teacher born	
300	Buddhism goes to Korea	Christianity becomes religion of Roman Empire (early 4th c.)
400	Buddhaghosa, Theravada teacher born	
		Augustine clarifies doctrine (354)
	Vasubandhu, Mahayana teacher born	
500	Buddhism goes to Japan	
600	Buddhism goes to Tibet	
800		Charles Martel crowned Holy Roman Emperor (800)
	Pagan B. kingdom, Myanmar (849–1287)	
1000		Split into Roman and Orthodox Churches (1054)
		First Crusades (1096–1099)
1200	Buddhism disappears from India	Thomas Aquinas
1500		Martin Luther initiates Protestant movement (1517)
1600		Pilgrims arrive in America (1620)
1800	First Buddhist Temple in Canada (1876)	
	Buddhists & Christians attend World Parliament of Religions in Chicago (1893)	
1900	Vietnamese monk's self-immolation (1963)	Second Vatican Council (1962–1965)
	Buddhist practice flowers in the West (1970s)	
2000	Dalai Lama receives Honorary Canadian Citizenship (2006)	

Appendix II

Buddhists in the World[96]

China • 250 million

Southeast Asia • 136 million

Japan • 85 million

South Asia • 24 million

Korea • 11 million

Other areas in Asia • 21 million

North America • 3.9 million

Europe • 1.3 million

Oceania • .7 million

Middle East & N. Africa • .5 million

S. America & Caribbean • .4 million

Africa • .2 million

Total worldwide • 527 million

---

96 Based on the 2012 Pew Research Center survey of Buddhists in the world; only the Japan number is taken from a Japanese government survey since it is more accurate, in my opinion.

Appendix III

Relating to Other Religions

As a Buddhist, I share the following basic attitude toward other religions:

1. Respectful: We respect other religions and honor their members' hopes to realize the goals of the religion.

2. Voluntary: We believe that the choice of religion is personal and voluntary.

3. Oneness: All people and beings are interconnected and make up the same world that we share. So, we share a lot more in common in our religious outlook than we think.

Among people of all faith traditions, there are basically five kinds of commonly held attitudes toward other religions.

1. One True Path (Exclusive): There is only one true path to the top of the mountain, and it is ours. Other religions aim to reach the top but are unable to get there because they are false.

2. One Complete Path (Inclusive): Many religions aim to reach the same mountaintop, but only our religion can accomplish that. Others are not false but are incomplete. So they must join and be included within our religion, which offers the only path for reaching the top.

3. Many Paths (Pluralistic 1): There are many different paths to get to the top of the mountain. And they are *equally valid* paths that lead to the same goal.

4. Many Mountains (Pluralistic 2): Unlike the former three, the religions are not different paths on the *same* mountain but paths on separate and *different* mountains. This view acknowledges the *uniqueness* of each religion but also the belief that when the seekers reach the top of their respective mountains their views are *similar* with much more in common than differences.

5. Different Peaks on the Same Mountain Range (Pluralistic 3): This position embraces the uniqueness of religions as in the previous position, yet regards religions not as separate mountains but as different *peaks* on the *same* mountain range. This view is, then, able to capture the truth that religions share not only the same earth but also the same aspiration to realize ultimate happiness and meaning as members belonging to the same human species.

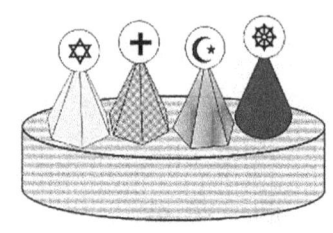

I take the fifth position (Different Peaks on the Same Mountain Range) because it respects not only the uniqueness of each religion but also acknowledges that members of each religion can reach the top of their respective peaks.

It also reminds us that the religions share the same space (Earth), have the same aspiration (salvation/liberation), and of the same species (homo sapiens). By taking this position, we believe that the many religions found in this country and the rest of the world can coexist in the spirit of mutual respect and active cooperation.

Appendix IV

Buddhist Holidays

THE FOLLOWING are the holidays that are common to most schools or traditions of Buddhism in America. They are mostly related to the major events in the life of Shakyamuni Buddha. It is interesting that the various denominations observe them at different times of the year.

The holidays specific to the various schools or denominations are not listed here, for they would be too numerous to name; readers are recommended to check with the respective traditions.

New Year's Day

Many cultural traditions have their own celebration dates, but in Canada they may observe the new year on January 1st in accord with the North American holiday. Others celebrate according to the lunar calendar, which usually falls in February.

Buddha's Birthday
April 8th

In Japanese based schools, it is often called "Flower Festival" to remind us of the joy and the abundance of flowers in the Lumbini Garden when he was born.

April–May

In Theravada schools, it is called "Vesak" and celebrated on the full moon of the fifth lunar month. Three major events in the Buddha's life are celebrated at Vesak: Buddha's 1) birthday, 2) Awakening or Enlightenment, and 3) passing.

Buddha's Awakening/Enlightenment
April–May

In Theravada schools, it is called "Vesak" and celebrated on the full moon of the fifth lunar month along with the Buddha's birthday and passing.

December 8th

In Japanese based schools, Buddha's Awakening is celebrated on this date.

Buddha's Passing

In Japanese based schools, Buddha's Passing is marked on February 15.

In Theravada schools, it is called "Vesak" and celebrated on the full moon of the fifth lunar month along with the Buddha's birth and Awakening.

Parents' Day

In the Vietnamese tradition, it is celebrated on the 15th day of the seventh lunar month as the day to express gratitude to one's parents.

PHOTO SECTION

WHEN WE KNEW we'd be publishing this book, we reached out to Canadian Buddhist centres and the media to find pictures that would best illustrate the breadth and depth of Buddhist practice here. Here are some of them.

Photo courtesy of Ken Tanaka

Above: Some Canadian Jodo Shinshu priests having fun at a district conference in Kamloops.
Below: A Rakusu ceremony with Lynda Gaudry Sensei at the London Zen Centre.

Photo courtesy of London Zen Centre

Above: Monks at Birken Forest Monastery near Kamloops, BC, begin their meditation with offerings to the Buddha. Their monastery has incorporated many environmentally forward thinking elements and the head monk, Ajahn Sona, is well-known internationally for his environmental work.

Below: Ayya Santacitta teaching a retreat at the Canmore Theravada Buddhist Community Meditation Group in Alberta. Ordination of women is an important issue for Buddhists around the world, and Canada is home to many strong teachers who are women.

Photo Section

Above: Members of the Creston Zen Centre in BC take on a building project. Physical labour (*samu* in Japanese) has always been an important component in Zen Buddhist practice. We're not sure what they're building, but it sure looks like they're having a lot of fun!

Below: Sakuraji Sangha members from the Creston Zendo travelled with their teacher, Kuya Minogue, travelled to Montana to bear witness at Standing Rock, along with many other environmental activists protesting the Dakota Access Pilpeline (DAPL), which would cut across First Nations water resources.

Photo courtesy of the Paramita Centrey

Above: Tibetan Buddhist monks at the Paramita Meditation Centre in Quebec City, QC, in a ceremony over a sand mandala.

Middle: The shrine at Karma Tekchen Zabsal Ling in Aurora, ON, just north of Toronto.
Below: Lama Tashi Dondup fills a Buddha statue with rolled up mantras for an alcove on the main shrine. The mantras are printed, dyed red on the edges, brushed with saffron water, then rolled and bound with four colours of ribbon. Extra space in the base of the statue is filled with incense dust and semi-precious gems. Then the statues are consecrated.

Photos courtesy of the John Negru

Photo Section

Above: An aerial group shot of congregation at the Thiên Hòa Vietnamese temple in Westlock, AB. The temple, also known as the Westlock Meditation Centre, is home to one of Canada's largest Buddha statues, 15 metres tall and weighing more than 21 tonnes.

Below: Young members of the Westlock Meditation Centre conduct a meditation class together. Vietnamese temples across the country are at the heart of some of our most vibrant Canadian Buddhist communities.

GEMS ❖ *Tanaka*

Above: Monks at the Arrow River Forest Hermitage near Thunder Bay, ON, practicing in the Theravada tradition.

Below: Rev. Master Koten Benson and others at the Lions Gate Buddhist Priory in Lytton, BC. They are members of the Order of Buddhist Contemplatives.

Photo Section

Above: Mahamevnawa Burmese Meditation Centre north of Toronto, ON. Gawa Ling is a Tibetan Buddhist retreat centre and organic farm outside McLure, BC, near Kamloops.

Below: Assembled monks and nuns from Toronto's Buddhist communities join together at Ching Kwok Buddhist temple on Bathurst Street for an investiture ceremony to welcome a new abbot, after the passing of the previous abbot, the much loved Venerable Wu De. The temple has been a strong financial supporter of Buddhist Studies at the University of Toronto for many years.

Photos courtesy of Chris Ng

Photo courtesy of Joyce Lam

Top: Dinner celebration of the first group of graduates from Emmanuel College's Buddhist programs at the University of Toronto.

Middle: Speakers at an conference hosted by the Toronto Centre for Applied Buddhism.

Bottom: A group chanting session.

Photo Section

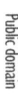

Top: Poster for HH Karmapa's 2017 Canada visit.

Right: Posters for Wesak in Toronto in the 1980s.

Below: First edition of the Journal of the Buddhist Council of Canada, 1987.

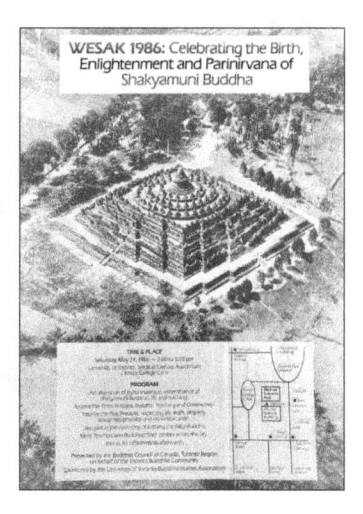

171

Sleepy monk statue, Cham Shan Buddhist Temple, Thornhill, ON..

Photo courtesy of John Negru

A planning session at the Manitoba Buddhist Temple in Winnipeg, MB.

Photo courtesy of the Manitoba Buddhist Temple

A group photo of the congregation at the Manitoba Buddhist Temple in the 1950s.

Photo Section

A young bhikkhu (Buddhist monk) at the Khmer Buddhist Temple in Maple, ON.

Photo courtesy of John Negru

Several of the teachers at the Manitoba Buddhist Temple's Sunday Dharma School pose for a snapshot.

Photos courtesy of the Manitoba Buddhist Temple

A young lady receives an offering from the Sensei at the Manitoba Buddhist Temple.

GEMS ❖ *Tanaka*

Top row photos courtesy of John Negru

Public domain

Photo courtesy of Thich Tinh Quang

Public domain

Top left: A fundraising embroidered patch from a Canadian EcoBuddhist Facebook group, with funds going to earthquake relief in Nepal.

Top middle + right: Buddhist sculpture in a cemetery in Richmond Hill, ON.

Left upper: Lotus Light Vancouver celebrates a successful charity drive.

Left middle: Bhikkhuni Tinh Quang of the Little Heron Zen Hermitage in Hamilton, ON promoting the Sakyadhita Association of Buddhist Women at a public event.

Left: His Holiness the Dalai Lama at the Vancouver Peace Summit, 2009.

About the Authors

Dr. Kenneth K. Tanaka spent his youth in northern California, in what has come to be called "Silicon Valley." After attending public schools in the city of Mountain View, he received his higher education at San Jose State Univ. and Stanford Univ. (B.A., Cultural Anthropology), a temple in Thailand (as a monk), Institute of Buddhist Studies (IBS), Berkeley, California (M.A., Buddhist Studies), Tokyo University (M.A., Indian Philosophy), and Univ. of California at Berkeley (Ph.D., Buddhist Studies).

He served as Associate Professor and Assistant Dean at IBS for 10 years and a resident priest for three years at the Southern Alameda County Buddhist Church (Jodo Shinshu) in northern California. During the early 1990s he served as President of the Buddhist Council of Northern California for several years. He, then, taught as Professor of Buddhist Studies at Musashino University in Tokyo for 20 years, 1998–2018.

As Theravada novice monk at Wat (Temple) Borwaneewais in Bangkok, Thailand, 1970.

Dr. Tanaka currently serves as Chairman of the Editorial Committee of the Chinese Buddhist Canon English Translation Project sponsored by the Society for the Promotion of Buddhism (BDK) as well as Adjunct Researcher at the Hongwanji Research Center.

He is the Past President of the Int. Assoc. of Shin Buddhist Studies as well as the Japanese Assoc. for the Study of Buddhism and Psychology.

Dr. Tanaka's publications in English and Japanese include *The Dawn of Chinese Pure Land Buddhist Doctrine*, *Ocean: An Introduction to Jodo Shinshu Buddhism in America*, *Amerika bukkyo* (meaning "American Buddhism"), *Buddhism on Air: Kaleidoscope of a Growing Religion*, and *Jewels: An Introduction to American Buddhism for Youth, Scouts, and the Young at Heart*. His English books have been translated into Japanese, Chinese, Portuguese, and Spanish.

Dr. Tanaka was the 2017 recipient of the 27th Nakamura Hajime Eastern Study Prize, awarded by the Eastern Institute and the Indian Embassy in Tokyo to scholars who distinguish themselves in the field of Indian and Buddhist studies.

Dr. Durgesh B. Kasbekar is a Vancouver based independent researcher. He serves on the Executive Committee of the Religion in International Relations Section of the International Studies Association (ISA), Connecticut, USA, and on the Board of Governors of the Steveston Buddhist Temple, Richmond, British Columbia, Canada. He is the recipient of the Royal Roads University Chancellor's award for the highest academic achievement in the Doctoral Program graduates of 2017.

He researches and writes on Buddhism in International Relations. He is working towards the formation of an Organization of East Asian, Indic and Folk Religions (OEAIFR) – an inter-governmental body which can have a Permanent Observer status at the United Nations and facilitate voting by East Asian, Indic, and Folk religions at the UN. He has presented on this topic in international conferences. Durgesh's idea of obtaining Permanent Observer Status for Buddhism at the UN was accepted as one of the themes for the Collective Buddhist Studies Manifesto. Several academicians on Buddhism presented the Manifesto at a Buddhist Studies round table at the Annual Conference of the American Academy of Religion held at San Antonio, Texas in November 2021.

Dr. Kasbekar was a delegate to the United Nations Summit on Sustainable Development held in Johannesburg; South Africa held in August-September 2002. He works as a Key Account Specialist at FedEx Canada. He is the recipient of the Canadian Award of Excellence for 2012 – the highest honor available to FedEx employees in the Canadian region in recognition for outstanding level of personal and professional commitment. He is the recipient of the FedEx Employee of the Month Award for January 2016, December 2019, November 2020 and the Everyday Hero Award for April 2022.

About the Authors

John H. Negru *(Karma Yönten Gyatso)* grew up in Montreal and became a Buddhist in 1970. He lived as a monastic for five years before returning to lay life. Since then he has been involved in many community development projects with Buddhist organizations in Canada.

During much of the 1980s, Mr. Negru was co-ordinator for the Toronto Buddhist Federation, and then Toronto coordinator for the Buddhist Council of Canada, complementary to his private practice, and career as a graphic designer and journalist.

In 2001, he left his career and previous teaching role in Ryerson University's publishing program to become a full-time Technological Education teacher in the York Region District School Board, where he served as a department head for sixteen years. During that time he launched several SHSM programs in Ontario, including one in Geomatics and one in Project Management. You may have crossed paths with those programs in your high school! Mr. Negru is also a Certified Associate in Project Management.

In 2009, he launched The Sumeru Press, Canada's only independent Buddhist book publisher and Buddhist news blog, and also launched the canadianbuddhism.info directory that currently comprises 550+ temples, sanghas, sitting groups, associations and retreat centres across the country. Sumeru has published many Buddhist books by authors from around the world, but focuses on Canadian Buddhist practice, particularly Buddhist responses to dealing with our Anthropocene overshoot crisis. The directory was last updated in 2022. There's probably at least one of those Buddhist centres in your home town!

In 2012, he conducted the first national sociological survey of Canadian Buddhist organizations, with assistance from the University of Toronto. The results were published in the *Journal of Global Buddhism* in 2013.

Mr. Negru is the author of several books on Buddhism and other subjects, including *Understanding the Chinese Buddhist Temple*, *Understanding the Tibetan Buddhist Temple*, and *Bodhisattva 4.0: A Primer for Engaged Buddhists*. He also writes a regular column for *Buddhistdoor Global* about environment and technology issues from a Buddhist perspective, and features for a variety of other periodicals.

Requesting Input from Readers

The primary author, Kenneth Tanaka, seeks questions and comments (including any errors, omissions, improvements, etc.) for his continuing effort to improve the book for future editions. Please send email to him at: chacotanaka@gmail.com

Index

A

afraid of death. *See* life problems.
aging, 78, 79
Ajahn Sona, 33, 164
Albert Low, 21, 72
Alberta, 20, 39, 67, 164
Alanis Morrissette, 21
American Oriental Society, 65
Anagarika Dhammadina (Anna Burian), 71, 72n
Anandabodhi. *See* Leslie George Dawson.
anger. *See* Three Poisons
Anguttara Nikaya, 112
anitya, 25
Arrow River Forest Hermitage, 168
attachments, 47, 77, 80, 81, 137, 139, 140
Aurora, 166
Awakening, aim of, 11, 24, 25, 27n, 110, 155
  Buddha and, 41, 45, 48, 117, 133, 161, 162
  karma and 89, 135
  meditation and, 23
  persons of, 49, 52, 53, 57, 85, 134, 144, 149,
  teachings about, 30, 37, 77, 108, 113, 124,
  nature of, 46, 47, 48, 81, 82, 83, 84, 86, 130, 136, 150, 151
Ayya Santacitta, 164

B

Bhante Mihita. *See* Suwanda Sugunasiri.
Bhante Saranapala, 32
Bhikkhuni Tinh Quang, 33, 174
Bhutan, 19
Birken Forest Monastery, 164

blessings or secular benefits, 87, 89, 145
Boat People, 69
bodhisattva, 45, 46, 47, 52, 172, 177
breaking up, *See* life problems.
British Columbia, 20, 33, 35, 65, 66, 68, 69, 72, 73, 176
Buddha nature, 52, 137
Buddha Shakyamuni, meaning of, 41
  ascetic practice of, 45, 46
  awakening experience of, 46, 47
  birth of, 42, 134
  childhood of, 42
  four excursions of, 43
  holidays for, 161
  leaving home of, 44
  life of, 41
  name of 41
  passing of, 49, 50, 51
  statues of, 37
  teaching of, 30, 31, 48, 51, 133
Buddhism, 17
  aim of, 11
  denominations & schools, 19, 22
  in North America, 7, 8
  in Canada, 9, 25, 27, 65, 71
  Living, 65, 66, 67, 68, 70
  Theravada, 28, 69, 71
  Mahayana, Vajrayana, 69
Buddhist Association of Canada, 72
  Council of Canada, 73
  Federation of Toronto, 72
  Heritage Day, 74
  Mission of North America, 67, 71
  organizations in Canada, 20
Buddhists, 17
  acquired, 22
  Burmese, 33, 55, 56, 69, 169
  Canada's, 69
  Canadian, 24, 25, 27

ethnic, 22
Euro, 22
Green, 32
inherited, 22
Japanese, 67
nightstand, 18, 22, 128
Shin, 66, 67
Jodo Shinshu, 67
Tibetan, 33, 34, 69, 154, 166, 169
Vietnamese, 69
bullying and prejudice. *See* life problems.
Burma, 51, 55, 56, 68

C

C.C. Lu, 33, 72
Calgary, 34, 38, 39
Cambodia, 19, 51, 56
Cambodians, 69
Canadian Buddhist Literary Festival, 32, 74
   Immigration Act, 1967, 26, 28
   Journal of Buddhist Studies, 73
   Multi-Culturalism Act, 1988, 26
   population, 17
Canadians of Chinese origin, 19
Canmore Theravada Buddhist Community Meditation Group, 164
Cape Breton, 29
Catholic Church, 26
Catholics, 35, 147
Cham Shan Buddhist Temple, 172
Chan Nhu, 72
chanting, 21, 23, 31, 60, 73, 153, 170
Charles Darwin, 24
China, 18, 69
Chinese, 18
   Chinese-Canadian, 19, 20, 67
   Buddhism, 61
   Buddhist Temples, 67, 72
   Chinatown, 67, 72
   Consolidated Benevolent Association, 67, 71
   from Vietnam, 69
Ching Kwok Buddhist Temple, 169

Chris Banigan, 34
Chris Ng, 31
Christianity, 17, 26, 41, 81, 128, 133, 134, 136, 157
Christians, 17, 24, 55, 60, 81, 157
climate change, 84, 111, 118, 156
convert Buddhists, 21, 22, 128
Creston Zendo, 165

D

Daimoku, 21
Dalai Lama, 23, 25, 28, 31, 32, 34, 36, 38, 62, 73, 113, 149, 150, 157, 174
Darshan Chaudry, 34
Daryl Lynn Ross, 34
Dharma Centre of Canada, 68, 72
Dharmadhatu, 72, 73
Dharma Drum Mountain Vancouver Centre, 68, 73
death, afraid of, 81, 130
   life versus, 59, 115, 116, 122
   suffering of, 78, 79, 124
   symbol or bringer of, 47, 141, 142
   transmigration through, 150
death of a family member. *See* life problems.
denominations or schools, 8, 19, 20n, 21, 22, 28, 51, 52, 53, 54, 58, 61, 62, 67, 13, 135, 138, 153, 161
Dianne Harke, 32
discrimination, 24, 34, 118
Dolma Tulotsang, 34
Doreen Hamilton, 34
Dr. B.R. Ambedkar, 34
Dr. Martin Luther King Jr., 28, 113
duhkha, 11n. *See also* suffering.

E

Edmonton, 39
Eightfold Noble Path, 77, 83, 85, 87, 90, 97, 98, 99, 110, 148. *See also* teachings.
Eileen Swinton, 33
emptiness, 40, 149
engaged Buddhism, 18, 22, 24, 59, 84
enlightened persons. *See* Awakening.

Index

envious of friends. *See* life problems.
ethics, 133, 138

F

famous Buddhists and sympathizers, 21, 23, 28, 31, 34, 97, 98, 150
five functions or aggregates, 79
Four Marks of Life, 91, 99, 100, 101, 102, 110, 111, 134, 148
Four Noble Truths, 49, 77, 78, 80, 83, 84, 85, 90, 91, 99, 133
France, 26
Frances Garrett, 33
Fritjof Capra, 23
fulfillment in life, 23, 90, 92, 95, 127

G

G.A.S. *See* Three Poisons.
Gaden Choling Tibetan Buddhist Temple, 72
Gawa Ling, 169
gems, 11, 12, 13, 14, 40, 82, 127, 156, 166
  Three Buddhist, 13, 29, 136
Geshe Khenrab Gajam, 34
Geshe Thubten Jinpa, 32
Glenn Copeland, 32
Glenn Mullin, 32
God: Christianity and, 8, 41, 81
  belief in, 17, 133, 136, 151
  Hindu, 48, 54
  judging, 114, 122
  spirituality and, 27, 118
gods, 67, 118
Gold Buddha Monastery, 68, 72
greed. *See* Three Poisons.

H

Halifax, 32
Hamilton, 33, 71, 174
  Buddhist Temple, 71
happiness, 80, 90, 102, 113, 146, 160
  and Nirvana, 81, 155
  foundations of, 114
  true, 78, 86, 108, 146
  wishing for others, 12, 24, 135

value of, 11, 13, 137
hatred. *See* Three Poisons
heavens, 42, 50
Henry Olcott, 55
Herbert Guenther, 32
here and now, 22, 24, 25, 108, 126, 144, 145, 147
Hinduism, 17, 53, 54, 55, 56, 134, 141
Hindus, 17, 18
history: Buddhism in Asia, 51-63
  in Canada, 65-74
Hong Kong, 68, 69
Honpa Canada Buddhist Mission, 67
humour, 75, 139, 141, 148, 149, 150, 151

I

ignorance. *See* Three Poisons.
impermanence, 81, 124, 126, 129
India, 24, 33, 37, 39, 41, 49, 52, 53, 54, 59, 61, 62, 68, 72, 134, 157
Indra's Net of Jewels, 127, 130
inferiority complex. *See* life problems.
insight meditation, 21, 23. *See also* vipassana.
interdependence or interconnectedness, 82, 125
Islam, 17, 18, 41, 56, 128, 133, 134, 136. *See also* Muslim.

J

Jade Buddha, 37, 73
Japan, 19, 26, 51, 58, 60, 61, 66, 67, 109, 132, 152, 157, 158
Japanese American, 132, 152, 153
Japanese Canadians, 38, 39, 67, 68
Jessica Main, 33
Jews, 17n
Jewish, 8, 18, 22, 24, 31
Jim Bedard, 21
Jim Carey, 21
Jodo Shinshu, 9, 66, 71, 152, 153, 163, 175
John F. Kennedy, 26
John H. Negru, 20n, 21
joy, 11, 42, 82, 104, 123, 161

Judaism, 41, 136

K

k.d. lang, 21, 31, 128
Kalu Rinpoche, 33
Kamloops, 164
karma, 84, 87, 88, 89, 90, 134, 135
Karma Tekchen Zabsal Ling, 166
Karmapa, 36
Khmer, 56, 69, 173
    Buddhist Temple, 173
King Ashoka, 24, 42, 51, 52, 54, 55, 157
Korea, 19, 32, 51, 58, 60, 68, 157, 158
Korean, 21, 34, 38, 60, 69, 72, 153, 154
Kuya Minogue, 33, 165
Kwan Yin, 35, 36, 67, 172
Kyoto, 8, 19, 67

L

Laat Sing Kung shrine, 71
Lama Tashi Dondup, 166
Lao, 69
Laos, 19, 51, 56
Laotian, 21, 56
Leonard Cohen, 21, 31, 128
Leslie George Dawson (Anandabodhi, Namgyal Rinpoche), 68, 72
Lien Hoa Temple, 70, 72
life problems, five principles of, 121
    losing a sports match, 122
    strict parents, 123
    breaking up, 124
    death of a family member, 125
    envious of friends, 126
    uneasy about being Buddhist, 127
    bullying and prejudice, 128
    uncertain about future work, 129
    afraid of death, 130
    inferiority complex, 131
Ling Yen Mountain Temple, 68, 70
Lions Gate Buddhist Priory, 168
London Zen Centre, 163
Los Angeles, 8, 19, 135
losing sports match. *See* life problems.
Lotus Light Temple, 67, 174

Lu Shengyen, 67
Lynda Gaudry Sensei, 163
Lytton, 35, 67, 71, 168
Joss House, 67, 71

M

Mahamevnawa Burmese Meditation Centre, 169
Mahayana, 45n, 51, 52, 53, 55, 56, 61, 69, 135, 157
Maitreya, 37, 73
Majjhima Nikaya, 108
Manitoba Buddhist Temple, 172, 173
Master Hsuan Hua, 33, 68, 72
meditation, 18, 21, 23, 27, 28, 29, 30, 33, 34, 55, 58, 60, 68, 83, 94, 95, 96, 97, 98, 115, 122, 133, 149, 164, 166, 167, 169
    Buddha's practice of, 45, 46, 50
    centers of, 20n, 69, 70, 73
    insight, 21, 23, 34. *See also* Vipassana.
    mindfulness, 21, 23, 28, 33, 37, 83, 90, 93, 94, 95, 96, 97, 99
metaphors: jewels, 9, 127, 130
    cliff hanger 142
mindfulness. *See* meditation.
Mississauga West End Dhamma School, 73
Mongolia, 32, 37, 51, 61, 62, 63n
monks and nuns, 22, 23, 24, 25, 36, 49, 51, 52, 53, 54, 58, 70, 90, 92, 96, 155, 169
    laypersons and, 52, 57
    Sangha and, 51
Montreal, 31, 32, 34, 38, 39, 72
    Zen Centre, 72. *See also* Albert Low.
    Zen Poetry Festival, 38
Muslims, 17, 18, 54
Myanmar. *See* Burma.

N

Nalanda College of Buddhist Studies, 73
Namgyal Rinpoche. *See* Leslie George Dawson.

Index

Nepal, 19, 33, 41, 62, 134, 174
Ngawang Norbu Kheyap, 34
Nibbana Sutta, 107, 156
Nichiren, 32, 61
Nirvana, 24, 46, 48, 50, 53, 81, 82, 83, 86, 100
Nishi Hongwanji, 66, 67
non-attachment. *See* attachment.
Nova Scotia, 20
now. *See* here and now.
nuns. *See* monks and nuns.

O

Ontario, 20, 39, 65, 68, 69, 72, 73, 74, 168
Order of Buddhist Contemplatives, 168
Ottawa, 32, 38, 39

P

Paramita Meditation Centre, 166
parents, 26, 42, 84, 101, 123, 124, 126, 127, 130, 162
Paul Keddy, 32
Pew Research Center, 17
Philip Kapleau, 72
philosophy, 25, 31, 40, 68, 102, 133
Physical-psychological components or functions, 78, 79, 80n
politicians, 8
Pope, 137
population: Buddhist, 17, 19, 26, 56, 57, 60, 145
  Canadian, 7, 17, 18
  Chinese Canadian, 19
  Christian, 17, 60
  Hindu, 18
  Jewish, 18
  Muslim, 18
  Sikh, 18
Prince Edward Island, 20
psychology and Buddhism, 23, 31, 33, 137
psychotherapy, 23, 153n
Pure Land, 9, 58, 59, 61, 175. *See also* Jodo Shinshu.

Q

Quan Yin, 67. *See also* Kwan Yin.
Quebec, 20, 31, 65, 69, 72, 166

R

racism, 38
Ray Innen Parchelo, 32
refugees, 33, 69,
reincarnation, 24, 62, 135, 141, 142, 150. *See also* transmigration, 24, 25
Rev. Master Koten Benson, 168
Richard Bryan McDaniel, 32
Right View, Intention, Speech, Conduct, Livelihood, Effort, Mindfulness, Concentration, 83, 90, 97, 99
Robert H.N. Ho Family Foundation, 74
Robert Wuthnow, 18n
Rod Burylo, 34
Rosemary Than, 33

S

Sakuraji Sangha, 165
Sakyadhita Canada, 74, 174
  International Conference on Buddhist Women, 74, 174
Samsara, 24
Samu Sunim, 34, 72
San Francisco Zen Center, 150
Saskatchewan, 20
Saskatoon, 32
Sau Fau Temple, 72
schools. *See* denominations.
science and Buddhism, 23, 24, 39
scriptures, 27, 48
Sean Hillman, 31
Second Vatican Council, 26
secularism, 26
Sensei Frank Ulrich, 35
Shakyamuni. *See* Buddha.
Shen Nong, 67
Senju Sasaki, 67
Shin Buddhism. *See* Jodo Shinshu.
Shin Buddhist temples, 68

Shirley Johannesen, 34
Shunryu Suzuki, 150, 151
Sikhs, 17
Sister Elaine MacInnes, 35
Soka Gakkai International Canada, 21
social action. *See* engaged Buddhism.
soul, 141, 148
South Asian, 19
spirituality/spiritual, 18, 27, 87, 88n,
    92, 96, 107, 123n, 153, 156
    and ethical foundation, 25, 61, 114,
        121
    and mindfulness, 93
    awakening, 23, 24, 41, 88n
    connection to body, 122
    happiness, joy, mental and, 13, 82,
        96, 127
    leader, 28, 43, 72, 151
    life, 44, 62
    mature person, 89
    overcoming desire, aversion and
        ignorance, 147
    path, 43, 47, 48, 79, 130
    seekers, 45, 92
Sri Lanka, 19, 51, 52, 54, 55, 56, 58,
    68, 72, 109, 157
Sri Lankans, 69
Stanley Fefferman, 73
Stories: Aesop's Greedy Dog, 78
    traditional Buddhist, 107, 115
    Who Moved My Cheese, 102
strict parents. *See* life problems.
stupidity. *See* Three Poisons.
suffering: Buddha's life and, 43, 45, 50,
    136
    cause of, 48, 79, 80, 81, 89, 100,
        114, 124, 137, 139, 147
    cessation of, 81, 112
    experience of, 78, 81, 84
    Four Noble Truths and, 77, 84
    free of, 42n, 108, 134
    nature of, 27, 48, 78, 80, 82, 113,
        123, 126
    overcoming, 23, 44, 59, 78, 82, 83,
        133, 136
    reducing, 11, 78, 84, 85, 90, 101,
        146, 24
Sumeru Books, 40n
    Guide to Canadian Buddhism, 20n
sutras, 53, 60, 134, 144
    Dhammapada, 93, 107, 108, 109,
        110, 137
    Flower Garland Sutra, 11, 53
    Junirai, The Twelve Verses of
        Bowing, 153
    Lankavatara Sutra, 143
    Larger Pure Land Sutra, 53
    Lotus Sutra, 13, 21, 53
    Nirvana Sutra, 53
    Perfection of Wisdom Sutras, 53
    Samyukta-ratna-pitaka Sutra, 111,
        117, 118
    Sandhinirmocana Sutra, 53
    Sutra of the Parables, 114
    Sutra of the Setting in Motion of
        the Wheel of Dharma, 49n
    Upama-shakata Sutra, 116
    Vimalakirti-nirdesha Sutra, 113
Suwanda Sugunasiri, 17, 22, 26, 72

T

Taiwan/Taiwanese, 19, 21, 51, 55, 58,
    59, 67, 68, 72
Tam Bao Temple, 70
Tam Kung Temple, 67, 71
Tantra, Buddhism and, 53, 54
Tanya McGinnity, 32
Tashi Lhanendapo, 33
teachings: Eightfold Noble Path, 40,
    77, 83, 85, 87, 90, 96, 97, 98,
    99, 110, 148
    Four Noble Truths, 49, 77, 78, 80,
        83, 84, 85, 90, 91, 99, 133
    Four Marks of Life, 91, 99, 100,
        102, 111, 134
    Three Learnings, 97, 98, 122
    Three Poisons or G.A.S., 79, 80, 81,
        85, 91, 110, 128, 134, 137, 147
    Three Treasures, Gems or Jewels,
        13, 61, 152
Temples (Burmese, Chinese, Korean,
    Sri Lankan), 69

Index

Tendai, 32, 61
Tenzin Gyatso, 28, 62. *See also* Dalai Lama.
Tenth Global Conference on Buddhism, 74
Thailand/Thai, 9, 19, 21, 51, 56, 57, 98, 146, 147
Thay Pho Tinh, 70
Theravada Buddhism, 51
   and meditation, 28
   and Southeast Asia, 21, 57, 135
   Burmese, 55, 68
   Cambodian/Khmer, 56
   Lao, 56
   Malaysian and Indonesian, 56
   Smaller Vehicle misconception, 52
   Sri Lankan/Sinhalese, 9, 54, 72, 157
   Thai, 9, 56
   and Vesak, 161
   Vietnamese, 59
   Canadian, 71, 164, 168
Thich Nhat Hanh, 25, 28, 37, 59, 70, 73, 95
Thich Thien Nghi, 70
Thien Hoa Vietnamese temple, 167
Thomas A. Tweed, 18
Thunder Bay, 168
   Buddhist Temple, 71, 168
Tibet/Tibetans, 21, 28, 32, 33, 34, 36, 39, 72, 166, 169
Tibetan Buddhism, 61, 62, 69, 150, 153, 154
Tiger Woods, 97, 98
Toronto, 8, 19, 31, 33, 34, 35, 37, 38, 39, 68, 69, 74, 135, 166, 169, 170
   Black Hat Initiation, 36
   Buddhist Church, 34, 68, 71
   Buddhist Federation, 33, 34, 72
   Buddhist Vihara, 34
   Centre for Applied Buddhism, 31, 170
   Congress of the Buddhist Council of Canada, 73
   Dharma Center of Canada, 68, 72
   Dharmadhatu, 71, 72
   Gaden Choling, 72
   Kalachakra Initiation, 34, 36, 73
   Mahavira Dhamma School, 72
   Vesak in, 32, 72, 73, 171
   Zen Buddhist Temple, 72
Tung Lin Kok Yuen Canada Society, 37, 68
Tynette Deveaux, 32
Tzu Chi Buddhist Compassion Foundation, 37, 59

U

uneasy being Buddhist. *See* life problems.
Union of Vietnamese Buddhist Churches in Canada, 70, 73
uniqueness of each person, 127
   of each religion, 159, 160
University, 29, 30, 153
   Concordia University, 34
   Dongguk University, 60
   McGill-Queen's University Press, 66n, 69, 72n
   Nalanda University, 53, 54
   Simon Fraser University, 73
   University of British Columbia, 33, 73
   University of Toronto, 30, 31, 32, 33, 73, 74, 169, 170
   York University, 73

V

Vajrayana, 32, 53, 69, 74, 135
Vancouver, 8, 19, 33, 34, 37, 38, 67, 71, 73, 135, 174
   Dharma Drum Mountain Vancouver Centre, 68, 73
   Gold Buddha Monastery, 68, 73
   Lotus Light Temple, 67, 174
   Nitobe Memorial Garden, 39
   Universal Buddhist Temple, 72
Venerable Bhante Saranapala, 73
   Chogyam Trungpa, 72
   Dr. Walpola Piyananda, 72
   Heng Chau, 68
   Heng Sure, 68

Hsuan Hua, 68
Lianci, 67
Lok To, 72
Shing Cheung, 72
Sing Hung, 72
Sing Hung Fa Shih, 72
Wu De, 169
Vesak, 32, 72, 73, 161, 162
Victoria, 67, 71
Vietnam/Vietnamese, 19, 21, 51, 58, 59, 157
   Buddhism, 9, 59, 162
   Canadian, 28, 69, 70, 72, 73, 167
   Refugees/Boat People, 69
   Thich Nhat Hanh, 25, 28, 37, 59, 70, 73, 95
   Thien/Zen, 59
   War, 28, 59, 157
Vimalasara/Valerie Mason-John, 33
vipassana, 21, 23, 34
Vivian Tsang, 34

satori, 150, 151
zendo, 165

W

Wendy Cage, 18
Westlock Meditation Centre, 167
women, 22, 23, 32, 74, 143, 164, 174
work. *See* life problems.
World Parliament of Religions, 65, 74, 157

Y

Young Men's Buddhist Association, 67
Yukon, 20

Z

Zasep Tulku Rinpoche, 34, 72
Zen or Chan Buddhism, centers of, 9, 72, 163, 165, 174
   history, 59, 61, 96
   humor about, 142, 143, 150, 151, 153, 154
   koans, 31
   Montreal Zen Poetry Festival, 38
   persons of, 31, 32, 33, 34, 35, 37, 150
   practice, 21, 28, 58

CPSIA information can be obtained
at www.ICGtesting.com
Printed in the USA
BVHW041435151022
649204BV00005B/15